SINGLE-MALT
WHISKIES
of
Scotland

The Islands

Inverness

Highlands

Aberdeen

SCOTLAND

Dundee

Perth

Edinburgh

Greenock • Glasgow

Lowlands

SINGLE-MALT
WHISKIES
of
Scotland

FOR THE
Discriminating Imbiber

James F. Harris

•

Mark H. Waymack

OPEN COURT

La Salle, Illinois 61301

✾

OPEN COURT and the above logo are registered in the U.S. Patent and Trademark Office.

© 1992 by Open Court Publishing Company

First printing 1992

Printed and bound in the United States of America.

Library of Congress Cataloging-in-Publication Data

Harris, James F. (James Franklin), 1941–
    Single-malt whiskies of Scotland: for the discriminating imbiber
  / James F. Harris and Mark H. Waymack.
      p.   cm.
    Includes bibliographical references and index.
    ISBN 0-8126-9212-8 (cloth). —ISBN 0-8126-9213-6 (paper)
    1. Whisky—Scotland. I. Waymack, Mark H. II. Title.
TP605.H36 1992
641.2'52'09411—dc20
                                                  92-21777
                                                    CIP

Contents

The Islands   123

Acknowledgements

The research involved in writing this book on single-malt whisky has been greatly facilitated by the generous co-operation of a number of people.

First, the managers of several distilleries were kind enough to open their doors to us during our visits to Scotland. We found these people without exception to be patient, courteous, and helpful teachers. Taking time out of their busy schedules, they escorted us about their facilities, answered the many questions that we had, and pointed out to us many of the other questions that we should have had. Particularly worthy of mention are the following distilleries and their various representatives, both in Scotland and in the United States: Aberlour-Glenlivet, Blair Athol, Bowmore, Bruichladdich, Glenfarclas, Glen Grant, The Glenlivet, Isle of Jura, Knockando, Macallan, and Rosebank. We thank these individuals and the companies they represent for their warm hospitality. Many thanks are also due to the Scotch Whisky Association for its co-operation. And special thanks go to William and Barbara Watson. J. Gordon Macintyre, proprietor of the delightful Clifton House hotel in Nairn, obligingly secured for us some of the distillery photographs reproduced in this book.

Our work has also benefited from several written works on whisky, in particular: *The Making of Scotch Whisky*, by Michael Moss and John Hume; *The Schweppes Guide to Scotch*, by Philip Morrice; *The Century Companion to Whisky*, by Derek Cooper; *Distilleries of Moray*, by Mike Seton; *Scotch Whisky*, by Simpson, MacDiarmid, FitzGibbon, House, Mackinlay, and Troon; *Scotland's Malt Whiskies*, by John Wilson; and *Scotland's Distilleries*, by Famedram Publishers.

While we have made efforts to provide accurate information concerning such matters as the ownership and operation of specific distilleries, the whisky industry is in flux. If the reader discovers any information that is no longer accurate, we welcome any such corrections.

A Door into the Extra-ordinary

Much of our lives is spent with the ordinary. We rise to our alarm clocks; we shower and dress; we eat our breakfast and go to work. A busy day ensues, and in the late evening, we retire. The alarm clock sounds the same each morning. It may serve to wake us up, but we really don't notice it, *per se*. The hot shower may feel good, but it is just like so many other showers that we have had. We may pay some attention to what clothes we put on—Do we need a tie today? Do the socks match?—but how often are we caused to marvel at the silk-worm who contributed to the tie, or the cotton plant that went into our shirt? The bowl of raisin bran serves as breakfast, but we tend not to pay much attention to it as a culinary experience.

Every now and then, however, we have one of those few experiences that jolt us, that enliven us, that rise above the ordinary. Such experiences lead us beyond the merely ordinary into the special, the extra-ordinary. These are remarkable experiences that are savored and that become objects of fond memories.

Such, for both Waymack and Harris, is the experience of single-malt Scotch whisky.

As academic philosophers who specialize in various aspects of and various figures in Scottish and English philosophy, we have both spent a considerable amount of time in Scotland and England beginning in the early 1970s. Waymack studied at both the University of Edinburgh and Exeter University, and Harris spent two years of post-doctoral fellowships doing research at Oxford University.

Living for any prolonged period of time in a foreign country is always an exciting time, for one becomes more conscious of the common, habitual parts of daily existence which are so routine and familiar that we all take them for granted until we are in situations where those things are different. For example, we Americans are frequently caught off guard by the simple difference that the British drive on the 'wrong' side of the road. Hence, we find automobiles coming at us in ways that we least expect. Indeed, a fellow American, having come to Oxford to study, was hit while crossing a street his very first day in Oxford! Clerks in retail stores in Great Britain (and on the European continent too) say, in a very friendly and routine manner, 'Thank you very much,' when a customer first hands over the money to pay for an item, in a tone which suggests that the transaction is completed even when there is change to be given back to the customer. The instinctive initial reaction is to think, 'But wait! I have some change coming back.' The clerk (or 'assistant') does, however, return with the change and the transaction is completed. But not before our routine is shattered and our attention is focussed upon trying to understand what has happened.

For Waymack, the first taste of single-malt Scotch was while hitch-hiking on a sunny spring day in the Scottish islands. A young physician, on vacation from Edinburgh, had picked him up on the Isle of Lewis and they had driven to a sandy beach where the Atlantic surf came crashing in. Jackets were zipped up against the strong ocean wind. And the doctor produced a flask of Talisker. Even on an otherwise out-of-the-ordinary day, this was an extra-ordinary experience. Peat smoke, rich malt, the salty sea, and fiery alcohol all exploded in the nose, mouth, and throat. Surprise, admiration, and wonder (the origins of philosophy, according to Plato) were all engaged. The desire to know and experience more was inevitable.

Harris remembers first noticing in English pubs that people would order Scotch whisky by strange, unfamiliar names which he could hardly pronounce. And they would drink the whisky neat—sipping it like brandy. His initiation to the world of single malts came when he prepared a traditional American Thanksgiving dinner to share with German and English friends in Oxford. Collecting all the ingredients for the traditional feast—including cranberry sauce and pumpkin pie—was an experience in itself. However, the teacher became the student when guests arrived with a special German holiday cake and with a single-malt whisky. The long afternoon and evening became a wonderful sharing of various culinary and cultural traditions. Long after the turkey and dressing and pumpkin pie were gone, everyone sat around the fire sipping their single-malt Scotch. Thus, the enjoyment of single-malt Scotch became blended with culinary enrichment, cultural adventure, and discovery.

Our first tentative adventures were startlingly revealing. Even though all of these whiskies were 'Scotch', they were each very distinctive. Some we liked and some we didn't. But we were hooked, and filled with the excitement of discovery of a whole new world of gustatory and sensory experience which we had not previously known even to exist.

Just as philosophers are eager to share their philosophical ruminations with each other, so we were bound to share our reflections upon single-malt whisky with each other. Thus began a gradual trial and error process which has led to a passion for single-malt whisky and a shared adventure which has now lasted more than fifteen years.

On our first trips back to the States from England, we brought suitcases full of single-malt Scotch, and we even induced our fellow travellers to bring back additional bottles for us. This was at a time when, in the larger metropolitan areas, one was lucky to be able to find two or three different single malts. We hoarded our treasure for months and years—periodically savoring them and sharing them with special friends. Americans, for the most part, had not even heard of single malts then, and few people had much of an understanding of what could be so special about a bottle of whisky that someone would go to the trouble to carry it half-way 'round the world. What we could find, we tried.

We returned to Britain in the late 1970s and early 1980s, and made it a point to do some 'field research'! Travelling with a letter of introduction from the Scotch Whisky Association and by contacting the different distillery managers, we were able to visit dozens of different distilleries. We have put thousands of miles upon rental cars, ridden numerous ferry boats, and got lost many times, in our efforts to visit the distilleries and their environs. But our efforts were rarely in vain. The Scots are enormously friendly, and everyone in our experience connected with the whisky business was very friendly and helpful. All of these people made our enterprise not only possible but very enjoyable as well.

About This Book

Philosophers have a long history of acknowledging to the reader that there are competing philosophical theories and explaining to the reader why he or she ought to pay regard to the author's new contribution. As both of us are academic philosophers, we have this habit ourselves, and think it a generally worthy habit. And since we are by no means the first people to write about single-malt whiskies, there would be no reason to make an exception in this case.

To begin with, tastes are somewhat subjective. Hence, it is not surprising that there is some disagreement amongst commentators, especially in terms of describing and evaluating single-malt whiskies. In that light, the judicious reader should welcome some diversity of voice, rather than relying upon the taste of only one person.

There are, though, some other differences between our guide and others that deserve mention and explanation.

First, we have noticed that some reviewers find it difficult or impossible to say anything bad about any single malt. We hesitate to speculate about the motives behind such a result. More importantly, it is *our* experience that some single malts are just not as good as others. In fact, some really belong only in blends. To borrow an analogy, they should be *vin ordinaire* rather than estate bottled. We are just a couple of academic philosophers whose only connections to the Scotch whisky industry are the ones which we tell the reader about in this book. We have no personal stake in the whisky industry. And, in good old American parlance, 'We call 'em like we see 'em.'

Second, some 'guides' to single malts assign numerical ratings to different whiskeys to measure their quality. While we recognize that some readers will be attracted to such a way of judging single malts, we regard this technique as, at best, an unfortunate over-simplification and, at worse, a gross distortion. On the one hand, it is impossible—both theoretically and practically—to rate very disparate items on a single scale when there is not a single set of criteria for evaluating the different kinds of things. Such a simple comparison commits what philosophers call a 'category mistake', that is, when characteristics or qualities from one category are inappropriately applied to another. For example, think of the impossibility of comparing the beauty of such disparate things as a sunset, a poem, a concerto, a flower, and a child. Are there any reasonable grounds upon which one could judge which is the most beautiful? Highland, Island, and Lowland single malts are all very distinctive whiskies. What makes something a typical or high-quality Island malt is quite different from what makes another whisky a typical or excellent Highland single malt. Even amongst the Island malts, the whiskies from Islay are quite different from those of the Orkneys. And even amongst the ones from Islay, there is remarkable variety; such that while there may be some family resemblance amongst the Islays, it is stretching matters to imagine there is a single 'paradigm' against which all Islay malts should be measured. So, it is just impossible to use mathematical precision to measure or judge the different single malts in a way which has any meaning at all. Finally, think of the aesthetic loss and simplification which results from trying to force works of art onto a mathematical scale. Suppose all of the great concerti, for example, or all of the paintings of the masters were 'rated' somewhere with particular numerical rankings. Think of the individual richness and variation and subtle nuances which would be lost. The same is true, of course, in trying to rate different foods or wines. This book is a celebration of a national treasure of Scotland, the richness of variety and difference and of the adventuresome spirit of those people who like to explore for themselves those differences. We intend this book to be one which is read with pleasure—not simply quickly consulted for a rating.

There are always some who, upon hearing of single-malt Scotch, automatically inquire, 'Which brand is the best?', and having obtained an answer, then conclude they know all they need to know on the subject. Discriminating imbibers will no more confine their attentions to one single malt than they would spend the rest of their lives re-reading just one novel or endlessly listening to one piece of music. Single-malt whisky is not merely a drink; it is a cosmos of gustatory sensations.

Third, some other guide books have profiles of more single malts than we do. This is typically done by reviewing what might be called 'brokered' single malts in addition to those marketed directly by the distiller. Large blending houses buy malt whisky from the distilleries to use in blending and own the whisky while it is aging. Now that the market for blended Scotch is depressed and the market for single malts is bullish, many of these whiskies, with no special mark of distinction, which would have previously gone into ordinary blends, are being marketed by the brokers as single malts at premium prices. Now there is nothing wrong, *per se,* with brokered malts. If one is avid enough, and wealthy enough, one might enjoy trying some of them. But our experience has been that they are very variable—what we find in one bottle may be vastly different from another bottle, even of the same distillery. Hence, what we might say about *our* bottle would be of very limited usefulness to the reader thinking about buying the bottle on the shelf. Furthermore, since the broker's own reputation is not on the line, there seems to be less concern with quality control. One bottles what one has, whether or not it is sound and desirable as a single malt.

For these reasons, we have chosen to focus our attention upon those distilleries that market their own single malt. We do make mention of some brokered malts, but only when there is, or has been, an 'official' bottling by the distillery to provide the substance for our entry. We have also left out some single malts that, though they may have been bottled by the distiller, are not marketed in a way that makes them available in any reasonable fashion.

In our view, less is sometimes more.

We have also passed over single malts produced outside of Scotland. Bushmills produces a lovely Irish single malt, though it is hard to find. Triple distilled, like Auchentoshan and Rosebank, Bushmills single-malt whiskey is light and soft, like a misty Irish evening. And the Japanese, having developed a passion for Scottish malt whisky, have now applied their energies to making whisky in Japan, doing their best to replicate the design and structure of Scottish distilleries. The results thus far have been mixed, some good, and some not so good.

On a related note, the reader may notice (as did one frustrated proof reader) that we consistently use the spelling 'whisky' rather than 'whiskey'. The British (and their Canadian and Japanese imitators) spell 'whisky' without the 'e'. Others, the Irish, and the Americans, make use of 'whiskey' with the 'e'. Perhaps another book will follow—one about American bourbon, whiskey with an 'e'—but *this* one is about single-malt *Scotch whisky.*

The Whisky Trail

As single-malt Scotch whisky has gained many fans in recent years, the Scots have made efforts to welcome the traveller intent upon visiting some distilleries and learning about Scotch whisky. By organizing our visits through the Scotch Whisky Association and by contacting the distilleries in advance, we were able to visit several distilleries which are not open to the general public and to get special guided tours of the facilities. But, many distilleries are now open to the public on a regular basis, and we highly recommend taking *The Whisky Trail,* a tour route put together through the co-operation of the Tourist Board with several of the distilleries, as a delightful and rewarding way of touring the Highlands. The trail takes one through several scenic locales with stops at a number of distilleries that have reception centers for guests. Maps and information concerning *The Whisky Trail* are available through a variety of different sources, including most travel agents and Information Centers in Great Britain.

The grape might be noble. And wine may have its charms. But there is a substance to single-malt Scotch, a ruggedness, complexity, and intensity that reflects its Scottish origins in barley, peat, and water. So if you are searching merely for truth, then perhaps *in vino, veritas.* But if you are seeking enlightenment, then, just perhaps, *in uisge beatha, illuminatio.*

May you enjoy Scotland's 'water of life' as much as we do!

Malt Whisky:
The Mystery of the Ages

John Barleycorn was a hero bold,
Of noble enterprise,
For if you do but taste his blood,
'Twill make your courage rise.

—ROBERT BURNS
JOHN BARLEYCORN

Many countries are identified closely with the fine products which they produce: crystal from England, silk from China, caviar from Russia. Perhaps, though, no other national product is as unique and distinctive or is so closely identified with the country which produces it as is Scotch whisky. The reason is that while whisky can be made anywhere, *Scotch* whisky (or simply *Scotch*) comes from Scotland and *only* from Scotland.

In Gaelic, the tongue of the ancient Celts, its name is *uisge beatha*, meaning 'water of life'. Shortened and anglicized, it becomes *whisky*, the national drink of Scotland. Its name captures the central position Scotch whisky occupies in the history and lives of the people of Scotland. For centuries, from the glens of the Highlands where the river Spey cuts through the heather-covered hills, to the Islands of the Inner Hebrides or Orkneys where the wind sweeps across the craggy and barren land, the making of Scotch whisky has been as much a part of life in Scotland as crofting and weaving.

The Scots did not invent the process of distilling liquor. Most experts agree that Irish monks brought the knowledge of distillation with them when they brought Christianity to the Scottish people as early as the fourth or fifth century A.D. Whisky quickly became an integral part of the life of the common people of Scotland, and the making of Scotch whisky became a part of every Highlander's common education. Births are celebrated with whisky; marriages are

1

consummated with whisky; and the virtuous are interred with whisky. Whisky was used to pay rent and to barter for other goods. Summers were for sheep herding and farming. Winters were for making whisky in the thousands of small, private distilleries scattered all over the country.

The first documented record of Scotch-making for public sale occurs in the Scottish Exchequer rolls of 1494, and two centuries later it had become a recognized article of commerce. Taxes were first imposed on Scotch by the Scottish Parliament in 1644. After the union of the Scottish and English crowns, the British Parliament, never loath to make financial use of its dominion, imposed a malt tax on Scotland in 1713. A long, bitter struggle ensued between the Highlanders and the excise men from the government, a struggle now immortalized in songs and stories. Finally, after a succession of different excise acts aimed at controlling illicit distilling, Parliament capitulated, and the act of 1823 contained far more reasonable tax rates which actually encouraged the illicit distilleries to become licensed. From these early beginnings, Scotch has become a major commercial and export product which is now known and appreciated all over the world.

Scotch whisky is the product of a process which combines the wisdom of the ages, the knowledge of a scientist, the skill of an artist, and the patience of Job. Never has so much been made from so little. Perhaps it was from making whisky that the Scots first earned their reputation for frugality.

The process appears so deceptively simple. It begins with the combination of barley with pure water to produce malted barley. A sugary liquid is extracted from the malt, and yeast is added to initiate fermentation. Then, in a process which is itself the distillation of hundreds of years of knowledge and experience passed down through generations, the fermented liquid passes through what is poetically called 'purification by fire'—distillation in the copper pot stills (often themselves a hundred years or more old) designed exclusively for this purpose. With the proper aging in oaken casks, the finished product, malt whisky, is what many people regard as the finest drink produced by human hand.

There are very important distinctions made by a connoisseur between the many kinds of Scotch whisky. When most people think of Scotch whisky, they usually think of one of the major brands sold abroad: J&B, Dewar's, or Johnnie Walker, to name only a few of the better ones. Even those who pride themselves on preferring a 'superior' brand of Scotch whisky think only of such brands as Chivas Regal or Johnnie Walker Black Label. All of these Scotches, however, are *blended whiskies,* a far cry from the *single malt.*

The overwhelming proportion of Scotch which is bottled and sold on the retail market is *blended whisky.* Blended Scotch whisky, made by mixing several different *malt* whiskies with a large portion of *grain* whisky (grain alcohol), was developed just over one hundred years ago. In 1831, Aeneas Coffey invented the *patent still.* Unlike the pot still, the patent still does not have to use only pure, malted barley. It can use almost any kind of ordinary grain, malted or unmalted, in addition to a small percentage of malted barley. Furthermore, the patent still operates continuously. Unlike the pot still, it does not have to be emptied and refilled after each distillation run, so the patent still can quickly produce large quantities of inexpensive, high-proof but relatively tasteless whisky.

The market for blended whisky really began to emerge in the 1870s, when the phylloxera blight wreaked havoc with continental vineyards. With the grapevines devastated, there was not enough wine to make sufficient brandy for the market. But with the technology in place to make blended whisky inexpensively, the whisky industry was prepared to fill the demand for spirits. Thus, blended Scotch became a commercial success on a grand scale.

A blended Scotch is made by taking the relatively inexpensive, blandly-flavored grain whisky and blending it with various of the richer, fuller-tasting, and more expensive malt whiskies produced by the pot stills. To produce a blend with the desirable characteristics of Scotch whisky, with a delicate balance of flavor, body, and color, and with the same flavor year after year, a blender may sometimes use as many as 40 or more different single-malt whiskies. While some blends use around 40 percent malt whisky many of the inexpensive brands may contain as little as ten or even five percent. The rest is grain alcohol from the patent stills. It is its inexpensiveness and its relatively mild or bland characteristics that give blended whisky its mass-market appeal.

Malt whisky, however, is the product of *pot stills*—curious-looking, tear-drop-shaped, copper stills used to make liquor from malted barley alone. A *single-malt Scotch* is pure, 100 percent malt whisky, produced by a single distiller. Single malts are the traditional whiskies, the products of history, heritage, and very little modern technology.

Sometimes, one may find a third family of Scotch—the *vatted* malt whisky. To make a vatted malt whisky, different single malts are mixed together without the addition of any non-malt whisky. These vatted malts are pure malt whiskies but are not *single* malts. Examples of vatted malts are Glenleven and Glenforres. While these vatted malts have much more interest and appeal than ordinary blended whiskies, it is the single-malt whiskies which occupy the undisputed place of pre-eminence in the world of Scotch whisky.

The single-malt whiskies are both more expensive and more strongly flavored than their counterparts. Perhaps for that reason they have never had the large mass-market appeal of blended Scotch. As a result, economy dictates that most of the malt whisky produced by the traditional distilleries is sold to the large blending houses to be used in their blends rather than sold as single-malt whisky. Many of the small distilleries cannot afford to market any of their whisky in the retail market as a single-malt whisky, so the distinctive color, aroma, and taste are lost except as a flavoring in a blended whisky.

In recent years, however, interest in single-malt whisky has grown dramatically. There are at present over one hundred malt whisky distilleries in Scotland, and around eighty of these are available in retail as single-malt whiskies. Retailers have responded to the growing interest, and now it is not unusual to find as many as 35 different single-malt whiskies in larger liquor stores. Furthermore, with the market for blended whisky in decline, the distillers have been more eager than before to offer their products as single malts. This has led not only to more distilleries being represented, it has also resulted in some distillers offering their single malts in different ages, including rare and expensive 25-year-old whiskies.

Single malts differ from one another dramatically in practically every aspect of flavor, body, color, and aroma. There is no good reason that we know why the exact combination of conditions in Scotland which result in the production of single-malt whisky could not be duplicated elsewhere. But, to date, all such attempts at duplication have failed. Exactly what it is that gives each single malt its unique and distinctive features is still very much in dispute. Some people say that it is the peat used in the fires; some say the water used in brewing; some say the shape of the pot stills; and some say the casks and the air where the whisky is matured. Whatever it is, single-malt Scotch whisky, like Scotland's famed Loch Ness Monster, remains one of those wonderful mysteries of life.

The process used by the different distilleries is practically identical and is no secret; the ingredients can be almost identical in neighboring distilleries. Yet, small, vague, and subtle differences become magnified during the processes of malting, distilling, and aging. The results are that each has its own character, taste, color, flavor, bouquet, and body. Even when a distillery has tried to duplicate a neighbor's product, the resulting whiskies are different. Defying complete reasonable explanation, it is as though being made *in a particular place* is itself one of the variables which makes each single malt what it is. The range of taste runs from the relatively bland and inoffensive to the very robust and distinctive. Preferences are very subjective and can be the source of many long and enjoyable evenings, tasting and discussing the relative merits of various single malts.

The tasting and comparison of various single malts can be a wonderful pastime. Much as wine connoisseurs enjoy rare wines, lovers of single-malt Scotch savor each drop. Purists say that single malts should be drunk only neat, and slowly, very slowly—much as a fine brandy. Some, who are more flexible, may allow a splash of water, most preferably pure spring water. Indeed, adding a little spring water may be quite appropriate with some of the rare single malts that are offered at virtually cask strength, such as Glenfarclas 104 proof. In such over-proof whiskies, a little spring water can help release aromas and tastes that otherwise would be all but locked up by the high alcohol content. 'Tossing off' a shot of single malt, adding ice, or mixing it with soda are very much frowned upon as a waste of a national treasure.

The appreciation of single malts, like the appreciation of the finer things in life—art, music, and gourmet food—requires an adventuresome spirit, an inquisitive mind, and the desire to experience excellence and variety. With single malts, an important part of the pleasure is gained from the adventure, thrill, and satisfaction of a new discovery and from sharing these experiences with one's friends.

The rich variety of single malts offers the opportunity for experimentation and subjective preferences which the relatively bland range of blended Scotches does not. The sampling—tasting and comparing—of single malts is best conducted as a social endeavor, since individual tastes and preferences differ so greatly. These single-malt whiskies, the traditional Scotch whisky, are one of the most unique, exquisite, and precious drinks known anywhere—*uisge beatha,* the water of life.

How Malt Whisky Is Made

There are four distinct stages involved in the making of malt Scotch— malting, brewing, distillation, and aging. These processes have remained largely unchanged for over a hundred years. Each stage represents a fascinating combination of science and art, knowledge and myth, history and folklore.

Malting

Scotch whisky begins with barley—pure barley with no other grains added or blended. Once, small distilleries used only the barley grown in the surrounding countryside, but now barley is often

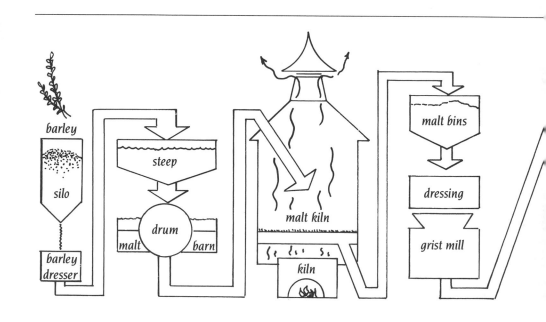

shipped from one area of the country to another or from other countries. Some distilleries still pride themselves on using only barley grown in Scotland. Others regularly use barley grown abroad, particularly from Australia and New Zealand to offset the limited growing season in Scotland. Modern technological advances in the malting process mean that regional differences in the barley can be minimized to the point of being inconsequential for the rest of the process.

The malting process begins with the addition of water to the barley. This starts the process of germination in the grain. Enzymes are produced which, in a later stage, will convert the starch of the grain into maltose, or malt-sugar. The barley is soaked in large tanks for fifty to seventy hours and then spread out to germinate on the floors of long, low buildings with low ceilings. To prevent the grain from over-heating and to ensure even germination, the grain is stirred ('turned') frequently during the eight to ten days of germination. This process is traditionally done by men using long, flat, wooden malting shovels. Through modernization, this process is now carried out in most malting houses by long, metal, mechanized 'fingers' in metal drums.

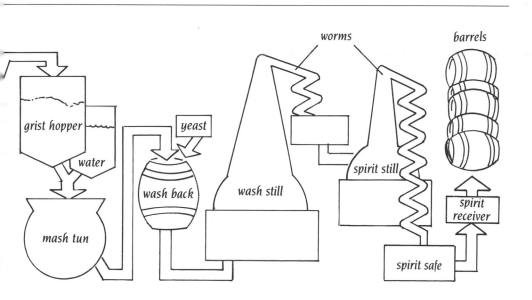

The germinating grain is watched carefully, and at the exact moment when the maximum amount of enzymes has been produced, but before the grain begins to sprout, the germination is brought to an end by spreading the wet barley on the floors of a large kiln and heating it. The kilns, the most distinctive buildings of the distilleries, with unique pagoda-styled ventilators on the roofs, are heated by burning peat, a very common fuel found throughout the Highlands and Islands. Peat, which is dug from the ground, is highly carbonized vegetable matter that has long been an important source of heating fuel in the Highlands and Islands of Scotland. After being dried, it can be burned, producing the distinctive, smoky odor which causes the unique 'peaty' taste of the single malts. Although some distilleries today mix coal with the peat, enough peat is still used to give the barley its unique aroma and taste.

The final step in the malting process is the grinding of the malted barley. The malted barley passes through a series of screens called a *dresser* and is cleaned of the small rootlets which are now dry and brittle and which will be used as cattle feed. The cleaned grain is then fed into a grist mill where it is milled to form *malt grist.*

In the past, malting was a part of the process carried out by the distilleries on their own premises, but now, most distilleries buy their barley already malted from maltsters who specialize in this stage of the production of malt whisky. The largest malting center, which supplies malted barley to dozens of distilleries, is The Group Maltings at Kirkcaldy on the east coast of Scotland, just across the Firth of Forth from Edinburgh. While distillers may have someone else actually do the malting, they still maintain strict control over the process. The distillers can specify in very exact standards precisely how much of the peaty flavor they desire in the malted barley.

Brewing

The brewing stage of the process of distillation turns the malt grist into a slightly alcoholic liquid which then enters the pot stills for distillation. First, the grist is mashed with warm water in huge, round, metal vats called *mash tuns,* each of which contains several thousands of gallons of the oatmeal-like mixture. The hot water causes the remaining starch to be converted into maltose—malt sugar—and dissolves the sugar. After several cycles of adding and then draining hot water, the malt grist has done its job. Having yielded up all of its sugars, it is taken off as *draff*. Since there is still some protein in the draff, it is dried and used as food for cattle.

The sugary liquid which remains is called *wort*. The wort is cooled before passing into the *wash tuns* (or *washbacks*)—deep, wooden vats. Now, brewer's yeast is added to the wort, and the fermentation process begins. Fermentation produces alcohol and carbon dioxide and is a very active process, causing the wash to froth and the wash tuns to vibrate. After 36 to 48 hours, when the alcohol produced by the fermentation reaches approximately five percent by volume, the yeast begins to reach the limits of its powers to convert efficiently the maltose into alcohol. This liquid is now called the *wash*.

Up until this point, the process of making whisky closely resembles the process of brewing beer, but as the wash enters the next stage, all comparisons with making beer are left behind.

Distillation

The wash is now pumped into the unique, teardrop-shaped, copper pot stills for at least two (and sometimes three) distillations. Some experts consider the exact size and shape of the pot stills to be crucial. When old stills must be replaced they are duplicated exactly, down to the dents and patches. The wash goes through two different stills, the *wash still* and the *low wines still* (sometimes called the *spirit still*).

The wash first enters the *wash still*. As the wash is heated, the ethyl alcohol, some water, and a variety of esters, oils, and other flavoring agents rise as vapor through the narrow neck of the pot still. The vapor enters a coiled, copper pipe, called the *worm*, where it condenses into the *low wines*, an impure distillate with a low alcohol concentration. After this first distillation, the low wines are approximately 20 to 25 percent alcohol, or 40 to 50 degrees U.S. proof.

The low wines next enter the *low wines still* or *spirits still* where distillation is repeated to eliminate undesirable impurities and to concentrate the alcohol. The vapor from the low wines still passes up through the neck of the still, enters the worm and is condensed. The condensed distillate passes from the worm of the low wines still through the *spirit safe*, a glass enclosure where the stillman can actually see the clear, colorless whisky. Using a hygrometer, the stillman can determine the specific gravity of the whisky, and by adding pure, distilled water, he can test it for impurities.

The first part of any distillation run, called the *foreshots,* contains many undesirable impurities and is usually directed back into the low wines still to await redistillation with the next run. Likewise, the last part of a distillation run also contains undesirable elements, including too much water. These *feints,* as they are called, are also directed into a receiver to be saved and then added to the next distillation run. The remaining residue in the low wine still, the *spent lees,* is a waste product. Only the middle part of the distillation run is regarded as pure enough to be selected as *potable spirits* which will become malt whisky. The judgment of the still man is crucial because too few of the aromatic and flavoring agents would produce a spirit more like tasteless vodka, whereas too many impurities would produce an unpotable or exceedingly diluted spirit

The clear distillate is diluted to about 60 percent alcohol by volume, and the process of aging begins. As the process of distillation is completed, the distiller is fortunate if he is able to produce two and a half to three gallons of whisky from each bushel of barley.

Maturation

All Scotch whisky must, by law, be aged in wood for a minimum of three years. In actual fact, nearly all Scotch is aged much longer than this. Most single malts are aged at least eight years, and most of the better single malts are aged at least ten to twelve years. Special bottlings are sometimes 15, 21, or even 25 years sold.

Maturation in oak casks is the stage in the production of single-malt whisky which many people think is most responsible for the distinctive characteristics of the different brands. The casks come in various sizes. The largest, containing more than 96 U.S. gallons, are called *butts. Hogsheads,* the next largest, contain around 54 U.S. gallons. *Barrels* contain at least 42 U.S. gallons. And *quarters* contain around 35 U.S. gallons.

Some distilleries (for example, Macallan) prefer used sherry casks for the aging process. The used wood is responsible for giving a rich, deep color to the fully matured single malt and the better distilleries go to much trouble and expense to get them. High quality, used sherry casks suitable for aging whisky are at such a premium that at least one distillery has the casks built and then 'loans' them to sherry houses in Spain to be used for aging sherry. After the casks are properly seasoned by the sherry, they are disassembled and shipped to the distilleries to be rebuilt and filled once again—this time with whisky.

Some distilleries (for example, Glenmorangie) prefer used bourbon casks, usually acquired from American distilleries, on the theory that the used sherry casks impart too strong a flavor. The used bourbon casks give the mature whisky a lighter, pale golden color. Since malt whisky aged in new oak casks acquires very little color or flavor from the wood, such whisky is sometimes colored, usually by the addition of caramel.

The casks are stored in long warehouses, usually at the distillery. The oak of the casks 'breathes', allowing between three and five percent of the whisky to evaporate each year. This has become known as *the Angels' Share*. With millions of gallons of whisky evaporating into the atmosphere during the course of a year, taking an invigorating breath of fresh air in Scotland acquires a completely different meaning. The evaporation makes the aging process an expensive one, but there are no cheap shortcuts past Father Time and Mother Nature.

As the young, raw whisky ages in the oak casks, it becomes mellow and smooth. The full flavor matures as the color deepens. The robust character develops ever so slowly as it takes on the undeniable characteristics of malt whisky. Young whiskies, five to eight years old, tend to be still quite fiery and harsh, however at ten to fifteen years, the mellowness of the oaken casks has somewhat softened the rough edges of the whisky, producing a smoother and more complex spirit.

In recent years, many distillers have made their single malts available in versions that have been aged 20 years or more. Since these whiskies command a very high price, it is helpful to know more about what happpens with these whiskies.

As the whisky rests in the cask, there is a slow, subtle interaction between the wood and the whisky. Some chemical compounds gradually break down; other gradually develop. Several years of aging are necessary to take the sharpness out of the raw spirit, but the results of aging 20 or 25 years and beyond are ambiguous. Some of the richest and most commanding of the whiskies can continue to improve to this point, becoming more round and smooth, taking on some of the characteristics of fine brandy as their peat and malt tones are softened. Weaker whiskies, though, can easily become woody and musty from too much time in the cask, losing many of their desirable features. Also, the aging brings out the best in some whiskies, for example, Macallan. But in others, the extra age results in the loss of their distinctive qualities; such is the case, in our view, with Laphroaig.

One question many people have is why the older whiskies are so much more expensive. Consider this example: A bottle of Springbank 24-year-old single malt, at cask strength (58 percent alcohol) was priced recently at $170, whereas a twelve-year-old version at normal strength cost around $34—quite a difference! Remember, first, that wood is porous, so a certain percentage of the whisky evaporates every year. In fact, somewhere between three and five percent. If we assume that four percent evaporates each year, when the whisky is 24 years old, the distiller would have less than two-thirds of the volume he had when it was only twelve years old. So he obviously has to charge more per bottle in order to break even. And don't forget, that the distiller could have sold the whisky at twelve years of age and banked the money, earning compounded interest each year. Indeed, his deposit at year twelve would have compounded to more than double its original value by year 24. Finally, the twelve-year-old is cut with water to be bottled at a fairly typical alcoholic strength of 46 percent alcohol. The 24-year-old, however, is unusual in that it is bottled at the cask strength of 58 percent alcohol. This alone means a price difference of more than 100 percent. Put it all together, and Springbank's revenue for its 24-year-old cask strength must be close to five times what it charges for its twelve-year old. This figure does overlook the fact that a significant part of the price of a bottle of whisky is government tax; but it also overlooks the fact that Springbank has warehousing costs each year. As a second example, a twelve-year-old Aberlour at $26 would be economically equivalent to its 25-year-old at $130. So there are good reasons why these extra-old whiskies are so expensive. Whether or not they are worth the additional expense depends upon the particular whisky and upon the drinker's own taste preferences.

Ninety percent or more of the fully-aged malt whisky is blended with other malts and with grain whisky to become 'blended Scotch'. However, with the reduction to proper proof strength, a small, select percentage of the mature whisky is bottled as single-malt Scotch.

However it is that single-malt whisky comes into being, whatever it is that makes the whisky of each distillery so uniquely different, there can be no doubt that it is one of the finest spirits ever distilled through the combination of human art and nature's bounty. With each dram of whisky one drinks, one thinks of its origins somewhere in the hills or shores of Scotland.

Choosing which single malts to review has been a difficult task. We have made an effort to include all of the single malts that we could find that are or were marketed by their distillers in a fashion that makes them reasonably available to the general public. For reasons already discussed, we have not devoted attention to whiskies that are only effectively available through brokers.

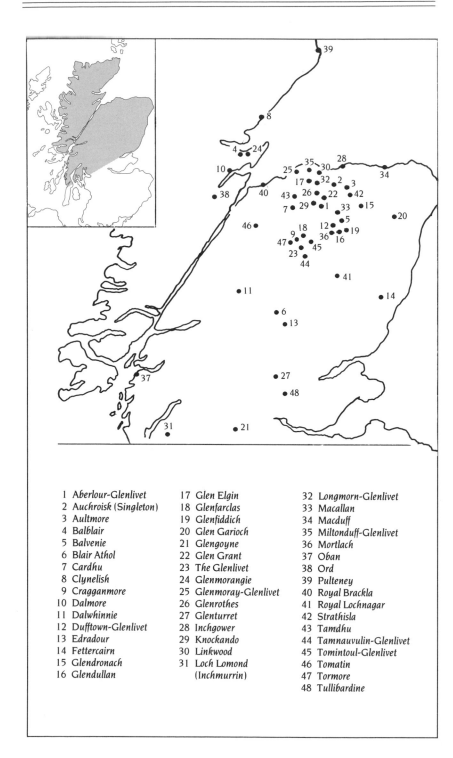

1 Aberlour-Glenlivet	17 Glen Elgin	32 Longmorn-Glenlivet
2 Auchroisk (Singleton)	18 Glenfarclas	33 Macallan
3 Aultmore	19 Glenfiddich	34 Macduff
4 Balblair	20 Glen Garioch	35 Miltonduff-Glenlivet
5 Balvenie	21 Glengoyne	36 Mortlach
6 Blair Athol	22 Glen Grant	37 Oban
7 Cardhu	23 The Glenlivet	38 Ord
8 Clynelish	24 Glenmorangie	39 Pulteney
9 Cragganmore	25 Glenmoray-Glenlivet	40 Royal Brackla
10 Dalmore	26 Glenrothes	41 Royal Lochnagar
11 Dalwhinnie	27 Glenturret	42 Strathisla
12 Dufftown-Glenlivet	28 Inchgower	43 Tamdhu
13 Edradour	29 Knockando	44 Tamnauvulin-Glenlivet
14 Fettercairn	30 Linkwood	45 Tomintoul-Glenlivet
15 Glendronach	31 Loch Lomond	46 Tomatin
16 Glendullan	(Inchmurrin)	47 Tormore
		48 Tullibardine

The Highlands

Twill make a man forget his woe;
'Twill heighten all his joy:
'Twill make a widow's heart to sing,
Tho' the tear were in her eye.

—ROBERT BURNS
JOHN BARLEYCORN

There are a few special places in the world where progress is not measured by how many changes occur—places where tradition, heritage, and the 'old way of doing things' dominate. The Highlands of Scotland is such a place.

Comprising nearly two-thirds of the land area of the country, this sparsely populated region is one of the most geographically and culturally distinctive areas of the world. It has produced most of the traditions, customs, and dress which are usually identified as being uniquely Scottish. Tartans, bagpipes, kilts, and the 'Highland Games' all originated in the Highlands, as did the Scottish clans themselves. The early Celts first settled in the Highlands, and even today, Gaelic, one of the world's most ancient languages, is spoken in many of the more remote areas. Gaelic proper names and words sprinkle the everyday language of the Highlanders. It is little wonder, then, that single-malt whiskies of the Highlands represent the oldest, largest, and best-known group of single malts.

With a short growing season, poor soil, and a large annual rainfall, the Highlands are particularly unfit for growing most agricultural crops; nevertheless, the Highlanders, as did their forbearers, still depend upon the land for their livelihood. Sheep produce mutton and the famous Scottish wool, and some of the finest grouse hunting and salmon fishing to be found anywhere attract sportsmen from all over the world.

As the Grampian Mountains rise out of the Central Lowlands, the terrain changes dramatically. From Aviemore toward the northeast, along the Spey Valley to Elgin, there are rushing streams bordered by lush trees and vegetation, grassy hills grazed by sheep and Highland cattle, and heather-covered moors. The blazing brilliance of the purple heather on the hillside in late summer is a lovely sight.

The largest collection of malt distilleries in this area is along the River Spey. These distilleries produce what have become known as the Speyside malts. While most of the malt whiskies from this area go to the blenders, several are bottled as single malts. As a matter of fact, more single malts come from this area than from any other area of Scotland. The single malts from Speyside have a full, robust flavor. With more body and a richer flavor than the characteristic Lowland malt whisky, these Speyside Highland single malts have less body, and less of the heavy, oily, peaty flavor of the Islay malts. Undoubtedly, some of the finest single malts available come from along the Spey.

The northern Highlands lie north of the Great Glen, a deep, natural geographical depression which cuts completely across the middle of Scotland from the Irish Sea to the North Sea. From Inverness and Fort William north to the Orkney Islands, the barren and windswept moors and peaks of the northern Highlands are one of the most isolated and desolate areas in Scotland, and perhaps anywhere in the world. This area is sparsely populated, with most of the inhabitants, as well as most of the distilleries, concentrated along the East coast. Only small villages and clusters of cottages are to be found in the northern Highlands proper. The single malts from this area are known as the northern Highland malts. The northernmost distillery on the mainland is Pulteney in Wick. Although generally not as well-known nor as highly-regarded as the Speyside single malts, these whiskies are genuine Highland malt whiskies and are often of very good character.

Aberlour-Glenlivet distillery, Banffshire

Aberlour-Glenlivet

(ABERLOUR, BANFFSHIRE)

Aberlour-Glenlivet distillery was founded in 1826 by John James Grant, one of the founding fathers of one of the most important families in Scotch whisky making. The original building burned and had to be completely rebuilt in 1892. The distillery is located in a beautiful, wooded setting on the banks of the River Lour, a tributary of the Spey River. In 1945, Aberlour-Glenlivet was purchased by the House of Campbell under which it operated until 1974 when it was purchased by the Pernod-Ricard group of France. The distillery was greatly expanded in 1973.

Like most other distilleries, much of the malt whisky produced at Aberlour-Glenlivet goes into the blending of the major brand of blended Scotch whisky of its owners—in this case, White Heather. However, unlike many distilleries, Aberlour-Glenlivet for many years also has produced a single malt in a variety of ages and strengths. At different times, Aberlour-Glenlivet has been available as a single malt eight, nine, ten, and twelve years of age and at varying proofs. Part of the variety is explained by the success of Aberlour-Glenlivet in foreign markets—particularly in France, China, and the United States. The twelve-year-old single malt at 43 percent alcohol is a whisky with a medium body and a nice, rich gold coloring. The aroma is well-balanced if a bit strong. The flavor is smooth with a distinct taste of peat. This is a very acceptable Glenlivet single malt.

Aberlour-Glenlivet is also available as a 25-year-old at 43 percent. It comes in a handsome wooden box which can be locked—perhaps a prudent feature, given the excellent quality of this whisky. The vintage dated 25-year-old is extraordinarily smooth and mellow, but with a rich, robust flavor. Along with only one or two other single malts, it ranks amongst the finest whiskies we have tried.

Auchroisk distillery, Banffshire

Auchroisk (The Singleton)

(Pronounced *awk ro isk*)

(MULBEN, BANFFSHIRE)

Owned by International Distillers and Vintners, and licensed to their subsidiary, Justerini and Brooks, Auchroisk was first opened in 1974. It sits on the banks of the Spey and draws its distilling waters from the well of Glen Dorie. Auchroisk is named for a local farm, the Gaelic word meaning 'the ford across the red stream'. The distillery has the capacity to produce some 1.5 million gallons per year.

International Distillers and Vintners may have first intended the distillery to augment its store of malt whisky for blending, but with the surge in demand for single malt, and the decline in interest in blends, it is not at all surprising that Auchroisk's malt is now being widely marketed as a single malt.

The Singleton, as this single malt is called, is bottled at 43 percent. Our sample was distilled in 1975 and bottled in 1988. This whisky possesses a full-bodied aroma. There is a light touch of peat, and the aging in sherry casks comes through on the nose. The taste, which fills the mouth, is full and well-rounded. The malt is evident, and there is a touch of nuttiness. The sherry tones are complemented by a slightly fiery presence. The finish lingers pleasantly. This is a very nice Speyside malt, a welcome addition to the 'notables'.

Aultmore distillery, Banffshire

Aultmore

(KEITH, BANFFSHIRE)

Located on the road from Keith to Buckie, in an area long used for illicit distilling, Aultmore was built by Alexander Edward of Sanquhar in 1895–96. In 1899, the company went public, but Edward remained as Managing Director of "The Oban and Aultmore-Glenlivet Distillery". Eventually the company gave up the pretense of being anywhere near Glen Livet, and dropped the appellation, becoming simply 'Aultmore'. Aultmore is now owned by the United Distillers and operated by Robert Harvey and Company Ltd.

Aultmore is available as a single malt at twelve years of age. It has a very lightly peated aroma. It is medium-bodied in flavor, more so than the aroma would lead one to expect. Some tasters have described it as 'smooth' and 'mellow'. Overall, it seems inoffensive and unexceptional.

Balblair distillery, Ross-shire

Balblair

(EDDERTON, ROSS-SHIRE)

Balblair is one of the older distilleries in Scotland. Although the present facility dates largely to 1842 and was greatly modernized and expanded around 1872, its lineage goes back at least as far as 1790, and perhaps as far as 1749. The distillery is located somewhat out of the way; it is in Edderton, near the Dornoch Firth, near Tain in Ross-shire. The vicinity is well blessed with peat, even by Ross-shire standards. Thus, it is no surprise that there is a long history of distilling, legal and otherwise.

The distillery, now owned by Allied Distillers, has a hospitality center with an educational tour followed by a heartwarming dram of whisky at the end.

Balblair single malt is available (though a bit hard to find) as a ten-year-old. It is quite light and dry, both in aroma and flavor, with a slightly flinty quality that is refreshing and pleasant.

Balvenie distillery, Banffshire

Balvenie

(DUFFTOWN, BANFFSHIRE)

Balvenie is the sister distillery to the well-known Glenfiddich distillery. Founded in 1892 by the same William Grant who also opened Glenfiddich, Balvenie lies just a few hundred yards away from Glenfiddich.

When first established, the distillery was named Glen Gordon, but the name was soon changed to Balvenie, taken from the nearby Balvenie Castle. Its five stills were increased to seven in 1965, and an eighth was added in 1971.

Balvenie still uses its own floor maltings. It draws its water from the same spring as Glenfiddich; and yet the two whiskies yield quite different results.

Our original sampling of Balvenie in the early 1980s was not all that impressive. The whisky was not as dry nor as peaty as the finer Highland malts, nor was it as polished, full in body or as robust as are, for example, Macallan and Mortlach. A recent sampling of what is now marketed as twelve-year-old 'The Balvenie Classic', however, struck us as an improvement over the versions of the early 1980s. The body is a bit fuller and more rounded; sherry tones are more noticeable. The finish is quite pleasant, long and lingering. On the whole, this has become a well-balanced, well-integrated whisky.

Blair Athol distillery, Perthshire

Blair Athol

(PITLOCHRY, PERTHSHIRE)

Blair Athol dates back at least to 1825, when it was first operated by John Robertson. The distillery was closed in 1932 and was acquired shortly thereafter by Arthur Bell and Sons who re-opened it in 1949 after extensive renovations.

The very picturesque distillery is located in the charming Highland town Pitlochry. The town is an important tourist center, being centrally and beautifully located with good access by road. It hosts a splendid theatre festival in the summer, and winter sports are the prime attraction in the winter. Edradour, another malt distillery, is located quite nearby.

Much of Blair Athol's whisky finds its way into the Bell's blends, but it is available as an eight-year-old single malt. Blair Athol is a light-bodied whisky. Its aroma is light, with just a touch of peat. The flavor is soft, light, and clean with no discernable aftertaste. This is a fresh, pleasant, but unassertive malt.

Cardhu distillery, Morayshire

Cardhu
(Pronounced *car doo*)

(KNOCKANDO, MORAYSHIRE)

Cardhu (sometimes spelled *Cardow*) saw illicit distilling as early as 1813, but a more proper distillery was built by a John Cummins in 1824. Then, in 1884, the distillery was completely rebuilt by Cummins's daughter-in-law, Elizabeth, approximately 300 yards from the original site, apparently because the lease on the original property was 'shaky'. In 1893, John Walker and Sons, of 'Johnnie Walker' fame, bought the distillery and it now resides in the United Distillers group. Extensive modernization and expansion took place in 1960, when two new stills were built along with a rebuilt mash-house, tun-room, and still-house. And the distillery now has furnished a visitor center.

Cardhu is Gaelic meaning 'black rock', probably a reference to the nearby Mannoch Hills which are very dark from a distance. One will frequently see the name anglicized in such a manner that it becomes *Cardow*. Many an unsuspecting newcomer to the world of single-malt whisky has thought Cardhu and Cardow to be two different distilleries. Even more confusing is that Cardhu is in Knockando, the town, where Knockando, the distillery, is also located. Tamdhu Distillery is also nearby. Cardhu is a Speyside malt whisky, but it is not regarded as a Glenlivet.

Malt whisky produced by Cardhu is heavily used in the Johnnie Walker blends, and a single malt is also produced at twelve years of age and 40 percent. The twelve-year-old Cardhu single malt is a very pale whisky (since no coloring is added) with a smooth and delicate flavor. It has a clean taste with a light aftertaste, and there is no flavor of peat—just a slight sweetness which is said to make it go particularly well with haggis. Cardhu comes in an attractive shorter, liqueur-shaped, cork-fitted bottle which might hopefully encourage people to accord this single malt the after-dinner status it deserves.

Clynelish distillery, Sutherland

Clynelish
(Prounounced *klyn leesh*)

(BRORA, SUTHERLAND)

The first distillery at this location, known as Brora Distillery, dates from 1819 when it was founded by the Marquis of Stafford who took the name Sutherland when he married into the Sutherland family and was named Duke of Sutherland. The Duke was closely involved in what have become known as the Highland Clearances, the forced removal of thousands of crofters from the interior Highlands. Many of the displaced Highlanders settled along the seacoast, and the Brora Distillery was part of a scheme to provide a local market for the grain of the smaller and poorer tenants. The distillery is located right on the coast, only a mile from Brora.

Distillers Company Ltd. took over the distillery in 1925, and it is now operated by Ainslie and Heilbron, a subsidiary of United Distillers. Like many of the other distilleries, Clynelish was closed during prohibition in the United States and during World War II. A brand new, modernized distillery was built adjacent to the old distillery and now operates under the name Clynelish. The old distillery now operates under the name of Brora Distillery, but it is closed at the present time.

Much of Clynelish goes to blending; however, a single malt is available in a variety of ages and proof strengths. The Sutherland Arms Hotel in Brora usually carries a nice selection of Clynelish single malts. The twelve-year-old Clynelish Finest Highland Malt, 40 percent alcohol, is a rich, robust, whisky with a full body. In many ways it is more like an Islay malt than a Highland one. There is a definite—almost strong—flavor of peat, but the taste is rich, smooth, and inoffensive. This is not a typical Highland malt and makes for an interesting comparison with the better Highland malts on the one hand and the Island malts on the other.

Cragganmore distillery, Banffshire

Cragganmore

(BALLINDALLOCH, BANFFSHIRE)

At the confluence of the Spey and Avon rivers lies Cragganmore, the distillery. Looking north, one sees the Spey flowing majestically. And to the south rises the hill, Craggan More, its peak not much more than a mile from the distillery, but rising some 800 feet above it to the height of 1,560 feet.

Cragganmore was built in 1869 by John Smith, after his having worked for both Macallan and Glenlivet distilleries. Gordon Smith, his son, inherited the works. His widow sold the enterprise in 1923 to Cragganmore Distillery Company Ltd. The facility was doubled in capacity in 1964 and now operates under United Distillers.

A delightful Speyside whisky, Cragganmore was until only recently unavailable as a single malt. United Distillers now offers it as a twelve-year-old. Its aroma is quite rich and complex with a freshness in it. It is medium-bodied. The initial taste has a touch of heathery sweetness that gives way quickly to an explosive smoky dryness that fills the whole mouth. There is a very pleasant, lingering finish. This is a distinctive whisky of high quality. Smith's experience at Macallan and Glenlivet carries through, and if one finds those malts pleasing, then one is bound to enjoy Cragganmore.

Dalmore distillery, Ross-shire

Dalmore

(ALNESS, ROSS-SHIRE)

Along the coast road which runs from Alness to Invergordon lies Dalmore Distillery. It is a beautiful setting overlooking Cromarty Firth and the Black Isle. Founded in 1839, Dalmore has been a part of the Whyte and Mackay Distillers, Ltd., since 1960. The water for Dalmore comes from the River Alness which flows for miles from the Loch of Gildermory over a gravel bed which acts as a natural filter.

Dalmore was closed during World War I, and the distillery was converted to the production of naval mines. It did not resume operation until 1922. Dalmore still produces its own Saladin maltings, and the distillery now boasts of eight stills capable of producing over a million gallons of whisky annually. The wash stills are short and rather broad at the base compared to most other pot stills, and the spirit stills have purifiers.

Much of Dalmore goes into blends; however, Dalmore has also been produced as a single malt at eight, ten, and 20 years of age. The twelve-year-old single malt is a full-bodied, smooth whisky. It has a deep, gold color and a nicely-balanced, rich—but soft—bouquet. The flavor has a hint of peat with a very pronounced finish which gives one just a wee bit of a bite of the strong and harsh weather of the northern Highlands.

Dalwhinnie distillery, Inverness-shire

Dalwhinnie

(DALWHINNIE, INVERNESS-SHIRE)

Dalwhinnie, the second highest in elevation of all Scotch distilleries, stands in the central Highlands at the entrance to Drumochter Pass. Although the distillery is of fairly recent vintage, dating only to 1898, the location is rich in history. In Gaelic, *Dalwhinnie* means a 'meeting place', referring to the crossroads where illicit whisky smugglers and cattle drovers frequently converged. This is also the site of Bonnie Prince Charlie's Jacobite army camp in 1745, as it assembled to march to the battle of Prestonpans. Dalwhinnie is now owned by United Distillers.

Dalwhinnie used to be difficult to find as a single malt. It was for a time bottled as an eight-year-old by the distiller. Then, for some years it was hard to find except as one of Gordon and MacPhail's Connoisseur's Collection. Now, however, United Distillers markets Dalwhinnie as 15-year-old single malt. The eight-year-old has a very light aroma and a rather dry, thin taste that seems to dissipate quickly. On the whole, it seems to be rather unremarkable. The 15-year-old is a bit more solid, with a touch of sweetness and a bit more smokiness than the eight-year, but still exceedingly light.

Dufftown-Glenlivet distillery, Banffshire

Dufftown-Glenlivet

(DUFFTOWN, BANFFSHIRE)

Dufftown-Glenlivet distillery is located in the beautiful Dullan Glen just outside Dufftown and a short distance from Mortlach Distillery. Dufftown is certainly the center of all of the Glenlivet distilleries, and some would say the center of all Scottish malt whisky distilling since there are no fewer than seven malt whisky distilleries in the vicinity. Dufftown is also a center of activity in the Highlands, and the Dufftown Highland Games are among the most popular in all of Scotland with individuals and teams frequently sponsored by the various distilleries. The Dufftown Highland Games are certainly highly recommended to visitors to the area in the summertime.

In 1933, Dufftown-Glenlivet was acquired (along with Blair Athol) by Arthur Bell and Sons Ltd. Thus, when DCL merged with Bell's to form United Distillers, Dufftown became a member of the extensive United Distillers' family. Already the top-selling brand of Scotch in Scotland, it is among the very few to have greatly expanded its export market in the last several years. In 1974, in order to increase capacity without running the risk of changing the traditional process at Dufftown-Glenlivet, Bell's built a sister distillery, Pittyvaich-Glenlivet, nearby, trying to perfectly duplicate the old pot-stills from Dufftown-Glenlivet.

The Dufftown-Glenlivet distillery was founded in 1896 and is usually regarded as a Speyside whisky although it uses water from the widely acclaimed Jock's Well, which is said to produce perfectly clear water—ideal for distilling.

Most of the whisky produced at Dufftown-Glenlivet goes into the blending process of Bell's many fine blended Scotches. However, Dufftown-Glenlivet is available as an eight-year-old single malt at 40 percent. As a single malt, Dufftown-Glenlivet has a well-balanced and slightly fruity aroma. The flavor is slightly peated and smooth, but the taste and body are somewhat thin, and the taste lingers mostly in the front of the mouth. Although this is a solid, middle-rated single malt, it does not rank amongst the truly exceptional ones.

Edradour distillery, Perthshire

Edradour

(PITLOCHRY, PERTHSHIRE)

Edradour Distillery, near Pitlochry, has the distinction of being the smallest distillery in Scotland. Since its founding in 1825, Edradour has had only one wash still and one spirit still. The annual production is only about 50,000 gallons.

Modernization in the form of electricity came to the distillery in 1947 and replaced the old water wheel for power. Otherwise, the process remains unchanged from what it was over a hundred years ago. Although the distillery is so small that visitors are welcomed only by advance appointment, it is certainly worth the necessary time and effort to see an operation which is very typical of what small distilleries were like in Scotland in the early nineteenth century.

Edradour has been owned for a number of years by William Whitley and Company, who in turn have been owned since 1982 by Pernod-Ricard, the French company, which operates in Scotland under the name Campbell Distillers Ltd.

Most of Edradour malt whisky used to go into White Heather, with only a small portion available as a twelve-year-old single malt through Gordon and MacPhail's Connoisseurs Choice series. Now, however, Edradour is bottled by the distiller at ten years old and 40 percent. Edradour ten-year-old has a nice golden color and a smooth, light but complex nose. The flavor is full-bodied, dryish, and malty, with a distinct taste of peat. The finish quickly becomes very light and a bit woody, the peatiness fades and is replaced by a noticeable sweetness on the tongue.

Fettercairn distillery, Kincardineshire

Fettercairn

(FETTERCAIRN, KINCARDINESHIRE)

Fettercairn is located near the village of Fettercairn, south and west of Stonehaven, at the edge of the Grampian Mountains. The early history is obscure, as with many whisky distilleries, but whisky was made at Fettercairn as early as 1824. At one time the chairman of the board was Sir John Gladstone, the father of the renowned Prime Minister. The distillery is now owned by Whyte and Mackay Distillers Ltd.

Old Fettercairn, as the single malt is known, is hard to find, since most of the whisky goes into blending, but there is a small quantity available as a ten-year-old. It is a very light whisky in both color and bouquet, as befits its eastern Highland origins. Its taste is dry, and the body perhaps a bit thin, but it is still quite smooth. This is a decent, light dram.

Glendronach distillery, Aberdeenshire

Glendronach

(HUNTLY, ABERDEENSHIRE)

The Dronach Burn supplies the pure Highland water from which Glendronach is distilled. The distillery still operates its floor-maltings; it still uses wooden fermenting tuns; and its stills are coal-fired—all signs of traditional whisky-making. This is a traditional distillery if ever there were one.

Glendronach was established in 1826 by a consortium of businessmen, but soon faced troubles when the distillery burned in 1837. With subsequent financial difficulties, the distillery became fair game and was acquired by a Walter Scott (though not 'the author of *Waverley*'!). For several decades in this century the Grant family (of the Glenfiddich distillery) owned the business. Its current owner, Teacher's, purchased the company in 1960, and is now owned by United Distillers.

Glendronach has entered the single-malt market quite aggressively in the last few years. First, a twelve-year-old was given preeminence over the eight-year-old. More recently, the twelve-year-old has been subdivided to offer the "original" and that "matured in sherry casks". The "original" is itself quite rich, with substantial malty notes as well as a noticeable sherry background. It is full bodied, with a full flavor that is complex. The finish is very nice and lingering, with a fresh, heathery tone. Not quite yet in the uppermost bracket, Glendronach "original" is developing nicely and deserves consideration.

Those who prefer a more mellow, rounded whisky will want to try the sherried version. The difference is not quite as marked as one might have expected, but there is a bit more roundedness, with a few more sherry notes at the first flush and then again as the lingering finish trails.

Thanks to Glendronach for offering the choice.

Glendullan distillery, Banffshire

Glendullan

(DUFFTOWN, BANFFSHIRE)

Glendullan, located just north of the distillery-rich town of Dufftown, was constructed by William Williams in 1897. There was a great deal of reconstruction in 1962 when a new still-house, mash-house, and tun-room were added. In the early 1970s, what is essentially an additional and separate distillery consisting of six stills was built. The business currently is operated by Macdonald Greenlees Ltd, and is owned by United Distillers.

Glendullan is available as a twelve-year-old single malt. It has an attractive aroma. Its feel in the mouth is quite smooth, but somewhat lacking in richness. There is a nice finish that hangs together rather than being scattered. Overall, this is a very pleasant whisky.

Glen Elgin distillery, Morayshire

Glen Elgin

(LONGMORN, ELGIN, MORAYSHIRE)

Glen Elgin distillery, located in Longmorn parish in Morayshire, was designed and built during the period of the 1890s when the industry was rushing to increase production capacity to meet public demand. The boom ended in 1898, when over-production led to the financial collapse of Robert and Walter Pattison, who had become major blenders. The ensuing scandal created a difficult period for a new distillery. Glen Elgin survived, however, and after passing through several different ownerships, it is now owned by United Distillers. The distillery was modernized and expanded in 1963–64.

Most of Glen Elgin goes into blends; however, as a single malt, Glen Elgin is available at twelve years and 43 percent alcohol. It has a pleasant but light aroma, and is medium-bodied with a somewhat sweet flavor. It goes down easily, but leaves an aftertaste which has a bit of a bite to it.

Glenfarclas distillery, Banffshire

Glenfarclas

(BALLINDALLOCH, BANFFSHIRE)

The Glenfarclas distillery is located just south of Craigellachie on the road from Grantown-on-Spey, at the base of Ben Rinnes. Founded in 1836, Glenfarclas is one of the oldest distilleries in Scotland and is also one of the few distilleries still under private ownership—J. and G. Grant Ltd. Five generations of the same family have owned and operated the distillery. Glenfarclas has a distinguished reputation for quality and excellence and is one of the few distilleries in the Glenlivet area (along with Macallan) which feels no need for the added recognition which would come from adding Glenlivet to its name.

The distillery has been enlarged and modernized at least twice— the last time in the early 1980s. Its six huge pot stills are now heated by gas and are kept in immaculate condition for the large number of visitors who visit the distillery. Water for Glenfarclas comes from the Green Burn and is piped down from the hill behind the distillery.

Glenfarclas goes out of its way to welcome visitors and has not only a large welcome center but also a display on the history and art of making malt whisky along with a large collection of single malts on display.

Glenfarclas is bottled at several proofs and at several ages. Most common is the Glenfarclas twelve-year-old which has a smooth, dry flavor. Not as full in body nor as peaty as some of the other Speyside whiskies, the twelve-year-old is still a very smooth and mellow whisky. While the twelve-year-old is aged mostly in sherry wood, the 15-, 21-, and 24-year-olds are all aged in 100 percent sherry wood. This difference, as well as the longer aging, is noticeable. The 15-year-old is certainly richer in aroma and taste than the twelve-year. The sherry wood is pleasantly noticeable, both in the nose and the mouth. This is a well-balanced, well-integrated whisky that ranks near the head of the class. The 21-year-old is even more exceptional. While some experts might say that additional aging past 12 or 15 years does little to improve a single malt, the 21-year-old Glenfarclas is a rich, robust, full-bodied, and full-flavored malt whisky. Still dry, but with more peat apparent in the flavor than in the twelve-year-old or 15-year-old, the 21-year-old is very smooth and mellow. With no harsh aftertaste, the whisky lingers delicately to be savored. This is an excellent whisky. Glenfarclas is also available as a 25-year-old. The whisky holds up well here. Though the oakiness is noticeable, the whisky is by no means woody or musty. It has, though, mellowed to the point where the peat and malt are quite subdued and the spirit resembles a fine cognac or armagnac. Indeed, it is perhaps closer to a cognac than it is to a typical Highland ten-year-old whisky. Glenfarclas also offers what must be the strongest malt whisky commercially bottled—an eight-year-old at 104 degrees proof. That translates into *60 percent alcohol!* This is *serious* whisky. The aroma is intense; malt and peat are evident, and it gently stings the nose. The flavor fills the whole mouth with a fiery explosion of well-rounded malt and the sensations of alcohol. Then there is a long, lingering finish. This is an unusual whisky that might be best enjoyed by slightly diluting it with either pure spring water, or even distilled water in a pinch.

Stills at Glenfarclas

Glenfiddich distillery, Banffshire

Glenfiddich

(DUFFTOWN, BANFFSHIRE)

Founded in 1886 by William Grant, the Glenfiddich Distillery has been owned and operated by the Grant family for over one hundred years. Located on the outskirts of Dufftown on the road to Craigellachie, the distillery is just a few hundred yards downstream from the Balvenie distillery and in the shadow of Balvenie Castle. The distillery was modernized and expanded in 1974, but the size and shape of the pot stills, like the ownership, have remained unchanged. The stills used by Glenfiddich are some of the smallest in operation in any of the distilleries in Scotland. Glenfiddich is one of the very few distilleries to do its own bottling on the premises.

Glenfiddich means 'valley of the stag'. This accounts for the prominent (and now very familiar) stag's head on the label of the unique triangular bottle. Glenfiddich is the largest-selling single malt in the world. It is well-known and easily recognized.

The Glenfiddich Distillery has a large, attractive welcome center for visitors and sells samples of its wares along with various souvenirs. The parking lot is usually full (including several buses) as thousands of people visit Glenfiddich annually. There is a slide show on the making of malt whisky and a tour of the distillery including a look at the bottling process.

Lighter in flavor and color than the more robust, fully-flavored Highland malts, Glenfiddich is a pleasant whisky. The aroma is light, even thin, and while the flavor is smooth, it lacks the full body and peaty flavor of a truly distinguished single malt. Without the strong, individual characteristics of the more robust single malts, Glenfiddich is frequently recommended to people who have been accustomed to blended Scotch and who are trying their first single malt.

For the serious collector, there is a special "Centenary" bottling of Glenfiddich which was done on Christmas Day, 1986, to commemorate (to the exact day) the one-hundred-year anniversary of Glenfiddich's operation. Also widely available is an 18-year-old Glenfiddich, available in a Spode ceramic decanter. A very rare 30-year-old Glenfiddich comes in an Edinburgh crystal decanter with a solid sterling silver stag's head, and is arguably the most expensive single malt produced that is available to the general public.

Glen Garioch distillery, Aberdeenshire

Glen Garioch

(Prounounced *glen geer* y)

(OLD MELDRUM, ABERDEENSHIRE)

Glen Garioch distillery is one of the oldest distilleries in Scotland, dating from 1797. It is located in the little village of Old Meldrum and has managed to keep many of the processes involved in the making of malt whisky unchanged since it first began. For example, Glen Garioch still does a large percentage of its own maltings, and these are done the old-fashioned way, by hand. In the past, Glen Garioch had some problems with its water supply, but these problems have apparently been solved by Morrison Bowmore Distiller Ltd, which now owns and operates Glen Garioch as well as Auchentoshan and Bowmore.

Glen Garioch has been recognized for spearheading experimental ways of conserving energy and reducing environmental impact. Currently, part of the heat produced during the malting and distillation is recycled back into the distillery and to heat glass greenhouses for growing tomatoes. The reports on this project are very encouraging, and it appears to be a great success.

Glen Garioch malt whisky has been used in blended Scotches for some time—principally Vat 69 and Rob Roy. It is available as a single malt at ten years old and 43 percent. This is a robust, full-bodied Highland malt with a distinct taste of peat. Its aroma and flavor are flowery. It is smooth and very mild to the palate, but it has a very strong and somewhat harsh, lingering finish, which comes as a surprise following the very mild initial taste.

Also now available is a 21-year-old in which the peatiness is more accentuated and the body fuller and more rounded.

Glengoyne distillery, Stirlingshire

Glengoyne

(DUMGOYNE, STIRLINGSHIRE)

Glengoyne Distillery, built and licensed in 1833, is located on the main road between Glasgow and Aberfoyle. The location of the distillery is at the bottom of a waterfall, at the foot of Campsie Fells—right on the imaginary line which separates the Highlands from the Lowlands. According to legend, Rob Roy hid in a tree nearby to avoid capture. Glengoyne is a very attractive distillery with a large reception center which welcomes visitors.

The distillery was owned by a single family for almost a hundred years. The Lang Brothers operated the distillery from 1876 until 1965 when the distillery came under the control of Robertson and Baxter Ltd. A major modernization of the distillery followed in 1966.

Much of the whisky from Glengoyne goes into blending; however, Glengoyne is available at ten, twelve, and 17 years of age. Though technically a Highland malt, Glengoyne is more like a typical Lowland malt. The twelve-year-old has a slight taste of peat with a nice bouquet. This is a smooth whisky with a medium-dark color which, although a bit thin in body, still goes down very easily. The taste is mellow and a bit sweet and lingers without the unpleasantness of a bitter finish.

The 17-year-old, is packaged in a bottle that vaguely resembles a pot still. The nose is quite light. The whisky is also light-bodied in the mouth, once again bearing resemblance to a good Lowland malt; nevertheless, it is warm and well rounded, with a faint and unusual (though pleasant) finish that lingers nicely. The flavor of the 17-year-old seems to hold together somewhat better than that of the ten or twelve-year-old.

Glen Grant distillery, Morayshire

Glen Grant

(ROTHES, MORAYSHIRE)

Two brothers, James and John Grant, built the Glen Grant distillery in 1840 in the village of Rothes. Making use of the waters of a nearby stream for cooling, Glen Grant draws its water from the Caperdonich Well.

James Grant's son, the Major James Grant, took control of the business at the death of his father in 1872. With great ambitions, he soon expanded the capacity at the Glen Grant distillery and built a second distillery across the road. This second facility was dubbed 'Glen Grant Number Two' and began production in 1897. The two distilleries were linked by a subterranean pipe which ran beneath the road dividing the buildings, and the whisky from both distilleries was called 'Glen Grant'.

The whisky glut of the turn of the century, however, forced Grant to close Glen Grant Number Two in 1901. Number Two was re-opened in 1965 and renamed the Caperdonich distillery, and the whiskies have since been kept separate.

Glen Grant was expanded in 1973 and again in 1977, and it now has a total of ten stills. Unlike the vast majority of distilleries which close down for the 'silent season' in the summer months, demand for Glen Grant is so strong that the distillery is kept in production nearly year round.

Glen Grant maintains a small visitor center. Helpful and friendly guides take the interested visitor about the distillery and explain the processes involved in the making of Glen Grant. As might be expected, Scottish hospitality happily dictates that the visit conclude with a dram of Glen Grant's delightful product.

Glen Grant-Glenlivet is available in a variety of strengths and ages, though it is increasingly difficult to find. The most commonly available is the twelve year, but 21- and 25-year-old versions can also sometimes be found. The twelve-year-old is a very smooth, medium-bodied Highland malt with a dry, nutty flavor. The 21-year-old is also a very smooth, medium-bodied whisky, but with more pronounced sherry tones in both the nose and flavor. The finish is distinctively dry and nutty.

The Glenlivet distillery, Banffshire

The Glenlivet

(GLENLIVET, BANFFSHIRE)

The Glenlivet, one of the most widely known and widely respected of Scotch whiskies, has a special place in the pantheon of Scotch—it was the first of the modern distilleries to be licensed.

The first appearance of the distillery was in 1747. John Gow, having participated in the failed Jacobite uprisings of 1715 and 1745, had decided that a change of name was in order. He thus became 'John Smith' and settled on a farm near Tomintoul. Given the marvellous resources at hand—pure water, quality peat, and home-grown barley—it was only natural to begin distilling. The distilling concern passed along to John's son, Andrew, who moved the farm and distillery to a different (though nearby) location. The next in line was Andrew's son, George, who inherited the family business in 1817. The Act of Parliament of 1823, requiring distillers to take out a license, faced the traditional opposition of most Highland distillers; but George Smith, with a canny eye to the future, took out the first such license in 1824. With the assistance and protection of the Duke of Gordon, Smith expanded the business and completely rebuilt the distillery. By 1839, he was producing somewhere around 8,000 gallons a year. 1850 saw the construction of a second distillery, named the Cairngorm. But in 1857–58, George and his son, John Gordon, built a new distillery at Minmore, closing the small older ones.

To protect its growing reputation from other distilleries who wished to associate themselves with the increasingly prestigous Glenlivet region, the Smiths managed to get legal protection in 1880, to the effect that they and *only* they could use the name *'The Glenlivet'*. Ten other distilleries were allowed the privilege of using *'Glenlivet'* only as a *suffix*.

The business passed along family lines until 1952, when through a merger it became the public company The Glenlivet and Glen Grant Distillers Ltd, and this company is now held by Seagrams.

The Glenlivet is a nice example of a light Highland single malt. Most widely available as a twelve-year-old, it is light in aroma, with a very subtle hint of heathery sweetness. Its body is nicely balanced, though not overpowering. The Glenlivet has more depth and character than Glenfiddich, though it does not have as much command and complexity as some of the more forceful Highland malts, such as Macallan or Mortlach. Everything considered, this is a very polished product.

Recently, 21-year-old Glenlivet has made its way into the American market. Sherry wood is more evident in the aroma than with the twelve-year-old. In the mouth it has a soft but firm body with tones of sherry, oak, and heather.

Of interest to the serious collector are two special bottlings of The Glenlivet. A limited quantity of 21-year-old is bottled in an exquisite Stewart crystal decanter, each bottle being individually numbered. This excellent whisky has a very delicate but firm bouquet. The additional years in the cask have resulted in a very refined flavor that is extremely smooth and mellow with just enough of a hint of peat for a wonderfully rich body. The Glenlivet was also bottled at 25 years of age in 1981 in celebration of the royal wedding of the Prince of Wales and Lady Diana. This whisky is now exceedingly rare and expensive.

Glencoe

Glenmorangie distillery, Ross-shire

Glenmorangie

(Pronounced *glen mor an gy*, like orange with a y on the end)

(TAIN, ROSS-SHIRE)

The Glenmorangie distillery was formally established in 1842–43, but both brewing and distilling were carried on at this site just north of Tain at least as early as 1738. Local folklore, in fact, suggests that alcoholic drink has been made here since the Middle Ages. When the Matheson brothers constructed the legal distillery in 1843, it had a capacity of around 20,000 gallons per year. The works were aquired by Macdonald and Muir Ltd in 1893, and now have an operating capacity of 600,000 gallons. Glenmorangie is now under Macdonald Martin Distillers.

Glenmorangie, named for the waters of the Morangie Burn, takes its brewing waters from the Springs of Tarlogie. It is said that the high mineral content of the spring waters contributes nicely to the finish of the whisky.

One of the first to market aggressively in the U.S., Glenmorangie is widely known and well-respected. It is bottled after ten years of aging in oakwood in the distillery's warehouse. Pale and aromatic, the whisky is light to medium-bodied, with a hint of sweetness and a gentle smokincss, followed by a mellow and rounded finish. It has wide appeal, and would be a nice choice with which to introduce a friend to single-malt whiskies.

Some Glenmorangie has been bottlcd by the distillery at older ages—18 to 24 years. It seems as though the distillery has not yet settled upon exactly how old the extra-aged Glenmorangie should be. The final results, however, are most likely to deserve attention.

Glen Moray distillery, Morayshire

Glen Moray-Glenlivet

(ELGIN, MORAYSHIRE)

Glen Moray-Glenlivet began operations at the site of an old brewery in 1897. It was bought by Macdonald and Muir in 1920 and was greatly enlarged in 1958, and thus is now a part of Macdonald Martin Distillers.

Only in recent years, as interest has grown in single malts, has Glen Moray-Glenlivet been available bottled as a single malt. In the 1980s, Glen Moray was widely found at ten years—unusually light in character, both in aroma and body. There is even a slight hint of flowery fragrance, and there is but the barest touch of peat. While the flavor does not fall apart in the mouth, it does dissipate rather quickly. More recently, the twelve-year-old has become standard. It still retains much the same character. Also available from time to time are extra-aged versions. A 25-year-old has been available—ours being distilled in 1962.

Glenrothes distillery, Morayshire

Glenrothes

(ROTHES, MORAYSHIRE)

The Glenrothes distillery was established in 1878 and began production in 1879. In 1887, the corporation merged with Islay Distillery Company to form the Highland Distilleries Company, which has owned and operated Glenrothes ever since. Built where there originally stood a sawmill, the works have been frequently modernized. Lauter tuns (adapted from European brewing technology) are used for the mashing, and new stills have been added. Thus, the capacity now stands at over a million gallons annually.

Most of the whisky goes for blending; so Glenrothes's single malt, bottled at eight years, is not very well known. It is a fairly typical single malt for the Glen Livet region. It is fairly light in body but with a soft, pleasant aroma (which has been called slightly fruity). Its flavor is smooth, with only a very light, lingering finish.

Glenturret distillery, Perthshire

Glenturret

(CRIEFF, PERTHSHIRE)

Glenturret distillery competes with Edradour for the honor of being the smallest (legal) distillery in Scotland. It was first licensed in 1775, though local records indicate that illicit distillers had been active in the area many years earlier. There were several changes of ownership in the subsequent century. Glenturret managed to survive the whisky glut, only to be closed in 1914. There was a brief respite in 1919–21, but by 1923 most of the machinery had been removed, and by 1927, the last of the warehouses had been emptied.

James Fairlie then acquired Glenturret in 1959, and under his personal direction the distillery was rebuilt in less than a year. Operations resumed in 1960, and by 1963 six new warehouses had been constructed. Under Fairlie's skilled leadership, capacity increased fivefold from 80,000 gallons to around 400,000. The increase in operations has not had a detrimental effect on the Glenturret's whisky. The eight-year-old version earned a Gold Seal in 1974 for matured whiskies under twelve years old in the International Wines and Spirits Competition. Glenturret is now a subsidiary of Cointreau, the French liqueur firm.

Glenturret is marketed in a variety of forms. Several different ages are available. Also, there are some versions that have been aged mostly in bourbon wood, and others aged in sherry wood.

The twelve-year-old is relatively light in color, as a consequence of being aged largely in bourbon casks rather than sherry wood. Yet it offers a full, pleasing aroma, rich in peat and carrying a touch of sweetness. Its flavor on the tongue and in the mouth is pleasant and rounded, almost buttery; good, but somewhat lacking in the complexity and body one is led to expect by the tantalizing aroma.

Glenturret is also available in eight-year-old, twelve-year-old, 15-year-old, and 21-year-old versions. Unlike many other 21-year-old whiskies, the Glenturret that we sampled still retains a good measure of a fiery character and entirely lacks the shades of sherry-tones one finds in, for example, a well-aged Macallan single malt. This is undoubtedly a result of the use of bourbon casks and new wood rather than the expensive and hard to find used sherry casks.

Inchgower distillery, Banffshire

Inchgower

(BUCKIE, BANFFSHIRE)

Inchgower may actually be traced to 1822–24, when John Wilson built the Tochineal Distillery near the mouth of the Spey River. Because the site was found to be unsuitable, the works moved in 1871 to the present site near Buckie, not far from the coast. It draws its water from the nearby Hill of Minduff which provides a far more reliable source than was available at the previous site. The operation was acquired by Arthur Bell and Sons in the 1930s, and is thus now part of United Distillers.

Inchgower is available as a twelve-year-old malt. It has a light aroma with a hint of sweetness to it. The flavor is light-bodied, with the same sweetness coming through. There is no particularly noticeable finish.

Knockando distillery, Morayshire

Knockando

(KNOCKANDO, MORAYSHIRE)

Ian Thompson built the Knockando distillery in 1898 on the banks of the River Spey, but as a result of the excessive competition and the whisky glut at the close of the last century, the enterprise was a failure. In 1904 the distillery was re-opened by W. and A. Gilbey, who bought it at the bargain basement price of 3,500 pounds sterling. More recently, Knockando was acquired by its present owners, Justerini and Brooks, a subsidiary of International Distillers and Vintners, in 1952.

The name Knockando is reputed to be borrowed from the Gaelic *cnoc-an-dhu,* meaning 'the little black hill'. However, according to Derek Cooper, a distinguished Scottish author, the correct derivation is from *cnoc ceannachd,* meaning 'the market hill'. The distillery is close to the river and, at one time, commanded quite a view of the surrounding valley, but the energetic efforts of the Royal Forestry Commission have succeeded in surrounding the distillery with pine trees which now obscure the view.

Knockando prides itself on using only Scottish barley in its whisky. The malt is lightly peated to Knockando's specifications and delivered to the distillery. Water for distilling comes from a spring uphill from the distillery, and water for cooling the condenser coils is drawn from the River Spey.

When Knockando is in production (usually from September through June), 16 workers operate four shifts which keep the distillery working smoothly around the clock. The four stills have an annual capacity of about 470,000 gallons, and Knockando has been working over the past few years at nearly 90 percent capacity.

Like most malts, the bulk of Knockando goes for blending, but a good supply is bottled as a single malt. Unlike most distilleries, Knockando prefers to identify on its labels the year of distillation and the year of bottling. With this practice, the consumer is aware not only of the age of the whisky, but its vintage as well. Knockando is usually bottled as a single malt at around eleven years of age.

Knockando is lighter than a typical Speyside malt. Its aroma is fresh, perhaps a bit soft. Its taste is light- to medium-bodied. This is a smooth, pleasant whisky that is very agreeable. Knockando is also available as an "Extra Old Reserve, twenty-one-year-old", in a distinctive decanter-style bottle. Our sample was distilled in 1964 and bottled in 1989. A little quick arithmetic should alert the reader to a peculiarity here. If a whisky were distilled in 1964 and bottled in 1989, how could it be *twenty-one* years old when by all rights it would seem to be *twenty-five* years old? What happened was that Knockando decided to introduce an extra old whisky in 1987. Anticipating using their 1966 vintage, they took out a license to import a whisky into the United States that was 21 years old. (U.S. import regulations require that the label state the minimum age of the whisky in the bottle.) But when the 1966 casks were opened, the still master decided it was not yet what they were looking for, it was not yet ready. So they tried the 1965 vintage, but that did not yet measure up to Knockando's aspirations. But when the 1964 casks were opened, Knockando knew that this whisky was what they were looking for. And so the first bottling of "twenty-one-year-old" was actually *twenty-three* years old. Knockando bottled the last of the 1964 vintage in 1990. After that the distillery will judge what other vintages, if any, are of just the right maturity and complexity for bottling as 'Extra Old Reserve'. Our sample has, indeed, benefitted from the extended aging. While still possessing that characteristic lightness of Knockando single malt, it has taken on more smoothness and complexity. Eschewing the robustness and strong sherry tones of, for example, the older Macallan and Glenfarclas single malts, Extra Old Reserve is a whisky of light, clean refinement.

Macallan: checking the whisky as it ages

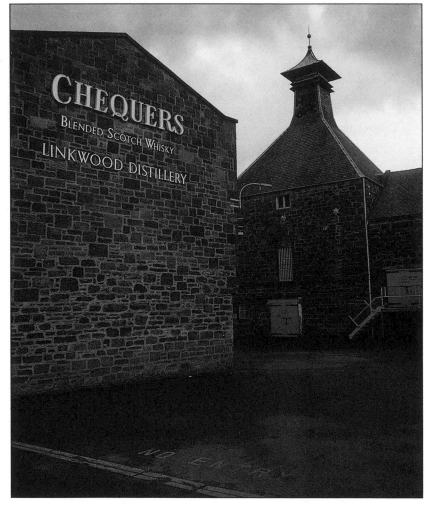

Linkwood distillery, Morayshire

Linkwood

(ELGIN, MORAYSHIRE)

Linkwood distillery is located just outside Elgin and was originally built as early as 1821 by its founder, Peter Brown. It was later rebuilt and expanded in 1863 and is now owned by United Distillers. The distillery is now a very attractive place to visit. It is located on a wooded site, and the Linkwood Burn from which the water comes for the distilling process runs along the side of the main building. Visitors can see the pot stills and watch the activities in the still house through large, plate glass windows in the front.

There are many great tales concerning the nonscientific and quasi-mystical process of distilling malt whisky, and one of the best involves Linkwood. It has been said of Roderick Mackensie—who was in charge of the pot stills and the process of distilling at Linkwood for many years—that he was so concerned about changing anything which might disturb the process and change the character of his whisky that he would not even allow a spider's web to be removed from the stillhouse. Whether or not the story is true, it certainly makes for a great tale.

Linkwood is bottled as a single malt at twelve years and at 40 percent alcohol. For a time, Linkwood also identified the year of distillation on the bottle. Linkwood is a classic Speyside single-malt whisky of high quality. It has a full, well-balanced aroma; and the flavor, though light in body when compared to some other Highland malts, has sufficient substance to avoid being thin. This very smooth whisky goes down very easily and leaves a pleasant, warm, lingering taste. Linkwood is a gem.

Loch Lomond distillery, Dunbartonshire

Loch Lomond (Inchmurrin)

(ALEXANDRIA, DUNBARTONSHIRE))

Loch Lomond was built in 1965, coming on line in 1966. On the banks of the River Leven, it is virtually on the line dividing Highland from Lowland, and should be classified as a Highland distillery. The distillery is built at the site of an old printing and cloth dyeing factory.

The single malt is called 'Inchmurrin', after an island located in Loch Lomond. It is now available as a twelve-year-old. The aroma is somewhat light and dry. The whisky is light-bodied, with an initial sweetness. It quickly separates into several disparate flavors. Overall, it is not very well balanced or integrated.

Longmorn distillery, Morayshire

Longmorn-Glenlivet

(LONGMORN, NEAR ELGIN, MORAYSHIRE)

John Duff, who also built Glenlossie and Benriach distilleries, began building Longmorn in 1894. It was brought into operation in 1897. In 1898 Longmorn was acquired by James Grant, and in 1970 the distillery became part of The Glenlivet Distillers family.

'Longmorn' is reputed to have come from the Welsh word, *lhangmorgund,* meaning 'the place of the holy man'. The distillery's water and peat both come from the nearby Mannoch Hills.

In some senses, Longmorn is quite traditional. It still operates its floor maltings and uses wooden washbacks. On the other hand, it has introduced quite new technology, such as a modern boiler which operates on 'waste heat'.

Longmorn is bottled as a 15-year-old. It is very aromatic, with noticeable maltiness. The whisky is medium-bodied, with a rounded, well-balanced feel in the mouth and a slight hint of nuttiness. It also has a pleasant aftertaste that finishes quite nicely. On the whole this is a fresh, complex, and well-integrated whisky.

The Macallan distillery, Banffshire

Macallan

(CRAIGELLACHIE, BANFFSHIRE)

The Macallan distillery lies just uphill from the River Spey, about a mile west of Craigellachie. The distillery was first licensed in 1824, but it is fairly certain that illicit distilling took place at Macallan much earlier. Macallan is located in a spot that was ideal for smuggling—near a ford of the river which was part of an old cattle trail leading south from the Highlands.

The distillery changed ownership several times in the nineteenth century, and was finally acquired in 1892 by Roderick Kemp, who made a number of improvements and expanded Macallan's already lustrous reputation. The distillery was modernized and enlarged in 1950 and again in 1959. Then, in 1964, a second, parallel distillery was built immediately next to the older still house.

Throughout these alterations, Macallan has maintained its excellence. For example, Macallan has persisted in using stills of the same small size and shape as its oldest stills. The refusal to economize by building larger stills has clearly maintained the quality of the whisky.

A second example has to do with the casks in which Macallan ages its whisky. Whisky producers have long used oak casks which have previously held sherry in which to mature their whisky. Oak is preferred over other woods because of its durability and its porous nature, which allows the whisky to 'breathe' as it ages, dissipating the more volatile elements of the raw spirit. Oak which has previously held sherry adds a special smoothness and color to the whisky which fresh oak does not impart.

For a long time, obtaining these used sherry casks was an easy and inexpensive proposition since sherry was fermented and aged in the sherry soleras in Spain in oak casks and then shipped to Britain. As it was expensive to return the emptied casks to Spain (and the sherry producers did not consider such used wood desirable anyway), the whisky distillers were able to acquire the used wood readily and cheaply.

In recent decades, the sherry producers have made more and more use of large stainless steel containers for shipping. Consequently, the supply of used, oak sherry casks has dwindled. As a result, many distilleries have resorted to buying used bourbon casks from the U.S., where, by law, bourbon casks must be made of new oak and used only once. Malt whisky which is aged in used bourbon casks, however, does not acquire the same color, roundness, and smoothness of flavor which sherry wood achieves and which so distinguishes The Macallan.

Rather than resorting to sherry concentrate to treat the used bourbon casks, as some distilleries are rumored to have done, Macallan approached the sherry producers directly and arranged to pay for the manufacture of oak casks to be used for making sherry which would then, after a few of years, be emptied and shipped to Macallan.

This arrangement has proven very successful for Macallan. Over the years, through controlled experiments with a variety of kinds of sherry, they have decided that the most preferable for aging The Macallan is oak which has contained dry oloroso sherry.

Attention to such details has made Macallan one of the finest of all single malts. About a third of Macallan's stock is now bottled as single malt, but as the demand for blended whisky has decreased, the proportion going into single malt has been gradually increasing. The Macallan is available at a variety of ages as well as vintages. It is widely available in the U.S. as a twelve-year-old. This is a very good whisky, full-bodied and smooth. The use of the sherry wood shows in the roundness of the flavor, but does not overpower the peat and malt of the whisky. It fills the nose and mouth with a very nice, well-rounded flavor. Macallan also markets some older whiskies that are even better than the twelve-year-old. There are vintage bottlings available, usually bottled after 17 or 18 years in the cask. We have had the 1962, 1964, 1966, 1971, and 1972 vintages. Each slightly different in their own way, these warm, mellow and well-rounded whiskies have consistently done well in all of our blind tastings. Either before or after a fine meal, they can put a fine cognac to shame. Finally, Macallan has made available a 25-year-old 'Anniversary' malt which is a truly excellent whisky. Very smooth and dry, it has gained a more subtle and complex character from the extra years in the wood. The additional years have not rendered the whisky 'woody', which would surely have been the case with a malt of lesser depth of character.

We have heard The Macallan described as the 'Rolls Royce' of malt whiskies. That appellation is not an overstatement.

Macduff distillery, Banffshire

Macduff (Glen Deveron)

(BANFF, BANFFSHIRE)

Glen Deveron is the product of Macduff Distillery, one of the more recent distilleries in Scotland. It was built in 1962. In 1980, it was acquired by General Beverage Corporation, of Luxembourg, themselves a subsidiary of Martini and Rossi. The name Glen Deveron is taken from the Glendeveron River from which the water comes for the distillery.

Glen Deveron is available as a 12-year-old single malt at 40 percent. This is a very light single malt without the full body and more robust flavor that one expects with the finer Highland malts. The bouquet is also 'thin' and there is just the hint of peat in the taste. Glen Deveron is an inoffensive malt; quite acceptable, but without the distinctive character of a truly fine malt.

Miltonduff distillery, Morayshire

Miltonduff-Glenlivet

(ELGIN, MORAYSHIRE)

Located about three miles east of Elgin (in actuality quite some distance from the River Livet), Miltonduff-Glenlivet distillery was established in the 1820s by Pearey and Bain. It sits on the barley-rich plain of Pluscarden, sometimes called 'the Garden of Scotland'. The distillery shares the site of Pluscarden Priory, now in ruins, founded in 1230 by Benedictine monks who were regarded as experts in brewing. The old mash house of the present distillery is said to have been the brew house of the Priory. The distillery was owned by Hiram Walker and Sons for many decades and operated by their subsidiary, Ballantine's. It is now owned by Allied Distillers. From small beginnings, the distillery was modernized and expanded in the 1890s, prior to the whisky glut at the turn of the century, and refurbished and expanded once again in the 1970s. Capacity is now near two millions gallons per year.

While virtually all of Miltonduff-Glenlivet used to go into blending (by no accident a large portion found its way into Ballantine's blends), it is now available as a 12-year-old. The aroma is quite light and sharp, with a hint of floweriness. The taste is light as well, with the slightest touch of peat. The finish dissipates quickly.

Mortlach distillery, Banffshire

Mortlach

(DUFFTOWN, BANFFSHIRE)

Mortlach Distillery is said to be built in the very valley where the Danes were defeated in 1010 by Malcolm II, the second king of Scotland. *Mortlach* means 'bowl shaped valley', and the Scots certainly put the valley to good use by breaking a dam holding the River Dullan and using the resulting flood to rout the Danes who were camped there. The distillery was founded in 1823 by James Findlater and thereafter went through a series of different owners. It was expanded and extensively refurbished and modernized in 1903 and was acquired by John Walker and Sons Ltd in 1923. It is now owned by United Distillers. Water for distilling comes from the nearby Conval Hills and from the Priest's Well.

Following a ruling by the EC Commission in 1977 which forbade dual pricing by distillers for United Kingdom and other EC countries, Johnny Walker Red Label blended Scotch was removed from the United Kingdom market, and a new brand, John Barr, produced by Mortlach Distillery, was introduced. John Barr has proven to be very successful on the home market, and because of its success Mortlach is now much better known than it was previously.

The malt whisky produced by Mortlach is much sought after by blenders. Much of it, of course, goes into John Barr, but several other blends regularly use whisky from Mortlach. Mortlach single malt is available at twelve years of age and 40 percent. This is a very full-bodied and very smooth whisky. There is only a hint of peat. The flavor is mellow and somewhat fruity. Mortlach goes down very easily and there is no harshness to the light finish—only a lingering smooth warmth. This is an excellent Highland malt. There is also a 16-year-old version now available, though it may prove hard to find. Special bottlings of Mortlach single malt distilled in 1936 and 1938 (both at 70 proof) are available from Gordon and MacPhail. These are very rare and very fine whiskies. United Distillers is apparently introducing a 16-year-old version of Mortlach. Whether that finds a market and becomes generally available remains to be seen.

Oban distillery, Argyll

Oban

(OBAN, ARGYLL)

Oban Distillery was founded in 1794 and is said by some to have the record for the oldest continuous operation of any distillery in Scotland. It is now owned and operated by John Hopkins and Company Ltd.

Oban lies on the west coast of Scotland. Primarily a fishing village, Oban also serves as the ferry departure for the Isle of Mull, where one may find the Tobermory distillery, the Isle of Islay, home of eight malt distilleries, and the Isle of Jura with one distillery. Campbeltown, with its distilleries, is a long day's drive southward from Oban, down the Mull of Kintyre. Given this location, it is difficult to classify Oban's single malt—is it Island, Campbeltown, or Highland? Given that the distillery is on the mainland and within the Highlands, Oban is counted here as a Highland single malt.

In the 1980s, Oban was offered as a twelve-year-old. The medium-bodied, twelve-year-old single malt, is produced at 43 percent. The aroma is complex, with a touch of sharpness. The rich, deep color without any strong sherry-tones suggests caramel coloring, and the flavor is smooth with a distinct touch of the smokiness and peat taste of the Islay malts, though by no means as heavy as the Islays. Twelve-year-old Oban single malt comes in an unusual octagon-shaped bottle with a glass stopper.

In the last few years, United Distillers has marketed a 14-year-old version of Oban. While not presenting a dramatic difference from the twelve-year-old, the 14-year-old does have a slightly more pronounced peatiness and the body is a bit heavier. We actually prefer the freshness of the twelve- year-old, but we suspect the fourteen-year-old will soon displace its younger sibling in the retail market.

Ord distillery, Ross-shire

Ord (Glenordie)

(MUIR OF ORD, ROSS-SHIRE)

For many years the site of illegal distilling, Ord was licensed as a legal distillery in 1838 by McLennan. After passing through a number of hands as well as expansions, Ord was acquired in 1982 by John Dewar and Sons, and is now in the United Distillers' family. It has a capacity of nearly a quarter of a million gallons annually. The distillery takes its water from a stream coming from Glen Oran and has a distinctive malting process during which heather is mixed in with the peat to flavor the malt as it dries.

Glenordie, as the single malt is named, is now available as a twelve-year-old. The color is rich and golden and the aroma is complex but mellow. The flavor is full-bodied and nicely balanced with a distinct taste of peat and a pleasant, lingering finish.

Pulteney distillery, Caithness

Pulteney (Old Pulteney)

(WICK, CAITHNESS)

Pulteney has the distinction of being the most northerly of all of the mainland distilleries. Located in Wick in the far northeastern, windswept corner of Scotland, Pulteney has been producing malt whisky since it was founded in 1826 by James Henderson. Nearby is Auldwich Castle which dates to the fourteenth century, a landmark for seamen known as 'The Auld Man o' Wick'. Pulteney was closed from 1926 to 1951, but it was purchased by Hiram Walker in 1955 and underwent a thorough modernization process during which the distillery was changed from coal to oil-fired heat. The distillery is now a member of the Allied Distillers group.

Much of the malt whisky produced at Pulteney goes to blending (particularly Old Smuggler), but a single malt is available as an eight-year-old at 40 percent. Old Pulteney, as the single-malt whisky is known, takes on much of the flavor of the north country. It has a rich, dark-golden color. Its flavor is somewhat heavier, more peaty malt than the average Highland malt, with a smooth, rich but dry taste. It is very distinctive and well worth trying.

Royal Brackla distillery, Morayshire

Royal Brackla

(NAIRN, MORAYSHIRE)

Supposedly, the official appellation 'Royal' can be used in Great Britain only because of some connection with a member of the royal family. Obviously, some of these 'connections' are much more tenuous than others. In 1835 King William IV chose Brackla to be served at state functions, and since then the whisky has been known as 'Royal Brackla'. To our knowledge, the only other single malt to have earned the designation of 'Royal' is Royal Lochnagar, which was the choice of Queen Victoria. The Royal Brackla Distillery, founded in 1812 by William Fraser, is located in Cawdor, just outside Nairn, beside the River Findhorn. Since the distillery no longer produces its own single-malt product, practically all of the single malt from Brackla goes into the blended Scotches produced by John Bisset and Company, such as Bisset's Finest Old and Bisset's Gold Label. However, a single malt is available through Gordon and MacPhail. Ours is a 19-year-old single malt at 40 percent alcohol. This is a deep golden whisky with a strong, full nose which has a definite peat character. The body is medium to heavy. The smooth taste fills the whole palate with a dry, sweet flavor. The finish is clean and dry. This is a very good single malt.

Lochnagar distillery, Aberdeenshire

Royal Lochnagar

(BALMORAL, ABERDEENSHIRE)

The Lochnagar distillery was built in 1845 by John Begg. His new enterprise was visited in 1848 by Queen Victoria and Prince Albert, during one of their stays at Balmoral Castle, which is only about a mile from the distillery. Lochnagar was appointed distiller to the royal household and was granted permission to be known as 'Royal Lochnagar'. Thus, the bottle for Royal Lochnagar carries as part of its label the designation, "By appointment to the late Queen Victoria and the late King Edward VII and the late King George V". A few short years ago, Lochnagar decided to revert to its original name, simply 'Lochnagar'. But it has now re-adopted its 'royal' appellation. While still operated by John Begg Ltd, the business was bought by Distillers Company Limited in 1916 and is now part of United Distillers.

Royal Lochnagar is bottled as a twelve-year-old single malt. It has the kind of aroma one might expect from a Highland malt—much lighter than the Island malts, but clean and with some substance. It has a nice flavor, with just a hint of sweetness, that fills the mouth and leaves a pleasant, lingering finish. It is a pleasant and attractive malt. Royal Lochnagar is also occasionally available in a "selected reserve" bottling of unspecified age.

Strathisla distillery, Banffshire

Strathisla
(Pronounced *strath i la)*

(KEITH, BANFFSHIRE)

Founded in 1786, Strathisla also claims (along with Oban) to be the oldest continuously operating distillery in all of Scotland. Earlier known as the Milton Distillery, its name was changed when Seagram's of Canada bought it in 1950. Located in Keith on the River Isla, the beautifully kept grounds, the unique pagoda roofs of the malting house, the water wheel, and the carefully tended flowers make Strathisla one of the most attractive distilleries in all of Scotland.

The four pot stills at Strathisla have been kept very small compared to the size of the stills at most distilleries. Two are fired directly by coal, and two are heated by steam. The water for the distillery comes from a private spring nearby whose waters some people claim have been used for brewing and distilling for over 600 years.

Strathisla (an important component of Chivas Regal) is bottled as a single malt in a variety of strengths and ages. In years past, the 15-year-old version was common. Now a twelve-year-old is being marketed by the distiller. This is a robust, full-bodied whisky. There is a distinct taste of peat, dryish at first, but then with a certain fruitiness and sweetness. Strathisla is not as mellow or as smooth as some of the very finest Highland single malts, but still quite respectable.

Tamdhu distillery, Morayshire

Tamdhu

(KNOCKANDO, MORAYSHIRE)

The Tamdhu Distillery was built in 1897 and has been owned and operated by The Highlands Distilleries Company Ltd since a year after it first started operation. The distillery is located at the foot of a small black hill alongside the Spey. Tamdhu has its own Saladin maltings which are used not only at Tamdhu but also at other distilleries owned by The Highlands Distilleries Company. The distillery has undergone an extensive modernization in the 1980s. The whisky is aged in oak casks in a bonded warehouse which is actually on the same site as the distillery. Tamdhu distillery was closed from 1927 until 1948; however, since it re-opened, Tamdhu has become a very popular single malt in Scotland and England.

Tamdhu is available at ten and 15 years old. The ten-year-old has something of a bite to it and seems a bit green, but the extra time in the oak casks of the 15-year-old takes some of the edge off the ten-year-old and produces a single malt of quality. The body is light without being thin, and the flavor has just a slight taste of peat.

Tamnavulin distillery, Banffshire

Tamnavulin-Glenlivet

(BALLINDALLOCH, BANFFSHIRE)

Tamnavulin-Glenlivet is one of the more recently established distilleries in Scotland. It was founded in 1966 by Invergordon Distillers Ltd which still owns and operates the distillery. The name *Tamnavulin* means 'mill on the hill' in Gaelic, and the name is appropriate because Tamnavulin was built alongside the River Livet near the location of an ancient mill in the foothills of the Cairngorm Mountains. The water for Tamnavulin comes from the River Livet and from a local spring nearby.

Invergordon Distillers produces its own blends, and Tamnavulin-Glenlivet has long been used in the production of the Invergordon's Glenfoyle Reserve. After 1974, it was produced as an eight-year-old single malt at 75 proof in a bottle that resembled a liqueur bottle; it was shorter than the usual whisky bottle and rectangular which might serve as a subtle reminder that a single malt ought to be treated more like an after-dinner liqueur than like a blended Scotch mixed with water or soda.

Now Tamnavulin-Glenlivet is generally marketed as a ten-year-old. It is sweet and delicate—both in bouquet and flavor—with little or no taste of peat. It is pale in color and light in body. The flavor is smooth with no aftertaste—just the lingering warmth of a well-made malt whisky. Although this is not a typical Highland Glenlivet, it is an interesting single malt—well worth trying.

Tomatin distillery, Inverness-shire

Tomatin

(Pronounced *to* **mah** *tin*)

(TOMATIN, INVERNESS-SHIRE)

Located alongside the A9, the main road from Aviemore to Inverness, Tomatin Distillery held the distinction, at one time, of being the largest distillery of Scotch whisky in all of Scotland. Following an expansion and modernization program which took 20 years and which was finally completed in 1975, Tomatin had 23 stills and the capacity of producing almost *five million* gallons of single malt whisky annually. It was also one of the most technologically advanced and most fully automated distilleries with as few as six men able to run the entire distillery. One person was able to control the entire process of distillation. Closed temporarily in the mid-1980s, Tomatin was then purchased by Takara, Shuzo, and Okura and was recently re-opened.

Despite the modernization and expansion, the process itself remained relatively unchanged. The water for Tomatin is still taken from a local burn, the Alt-na-frith, which originates in the nearby Monadhliath Mountains. The product itself was used by many of the principle blending houses for blended brands as well as being used in Tomatin's own blends. As a single malt, Tomatin is sold in a ten-year-old version that has many of the characteristics of a Glenlivet. It is light bodied with a smooth flavor and not much aftertaste. There is definitely a stronger taste of peat than in most Glenlivets.

Tomintoul distillery, Banffshire

Tomintoul-Glenlivet

(Pronounced *tom in towl*)

(BALLINDALLOCH, BANFFSHIRE)

Tomintoul-Glenlivet, reputedly the highest elevated of all Scottish distilleries, is located a few miles north of the town of Tomintoul. Its water for distilling comes from the Ballantruan Spring. Built in the 1960s as a joint venture of two Glasgow-based whisky brokerage houses, Tomintoul-Glenlivet came into production in 1965. Its production capacity stands at around a million gallons per year. The distillery is now owned by Whyte and Mackay.

Tomintoul-Glenlivet is available as a twelve-year-old. The aroma is faint and a bit thin. The taste is clean and light, though a bit sharp on the tip of the tongue; there is but a faint finish.

Tormore distillery, Morayshire

Tormore

(ADVIE, GRANTOWN-ON-SPEY)

Relatively high in the hills, in a remote location of rock, bracken, and heather, lies Tormore. Designed by Albert Richardson, a renowned British architect, Tormore was completed and brought into production in 1959–60. Not surprisingly, its granite buildings display an architectural creativity, flair, and whimsy not evident in other distilleries. There is even a clock with carillon chimes. Originally owned by Long John International, it is now held by Allied Distillers.

Most of Tormore's output goes into blending, but some is bottled at five and ten years as a single malt. Despite its modern facilities, Tormore fits with ease into the Speyside family of whiskies. The ten-year-old has a light, but not at all thin, aroma. Its flavor is pleasant, a bit dry, and well rounded—indeed, it seems to 'roll' in the mouth. And there is a pleasant, well balanced, and sustained finish.

Tullibardine distillery, Perthshire

Tullibardine

(BLACKFORD, PERTHSHIRE)

Built upon the grounds of a seventeenth-century brewery, Tullibardine was built in 1949 according to the design of W. Delmé Evans. Commissioned by William S. Scott Ltd, the distillery was acquired by Brodie Hepburn Ltd in 1954. Its present owners, Invergordon, bought the facility in 1972, and then modernized the plant, doubling its capacity to four stills in 1974.

The distillery is in the Ochil Hills. The Moor of Tullibardine is nearby, whence the distillery receives its water, the excellence of which is considered the reason for the former brewery's good repute.

Tullibardine is bottled as a ten-year-old single malt. The aroma is light, even by Highland standards. The flavor is clean, though slightly sweetish, with perhaps a hint of heather. And there is a delicate but lengthy finish.

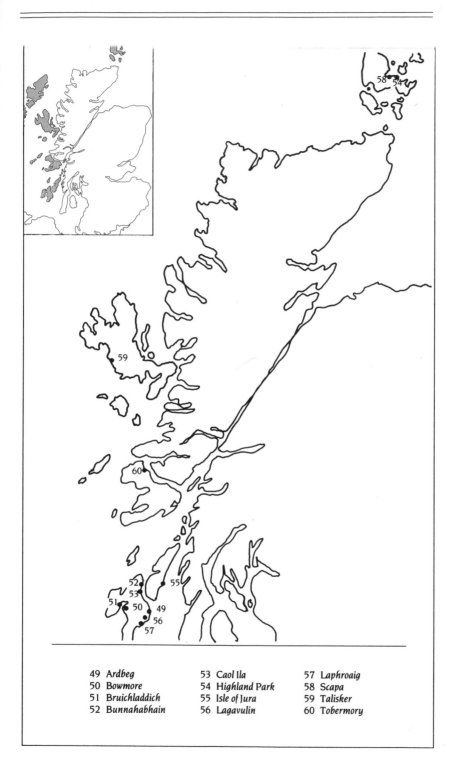

49 Ardbeg	53 Caol Ila	57 Laphroaig
50 Bowmore	54 Highland Park	58 Scapa
51 Bruichladdich	55 Isle of Jura	59 Talisker
52 Bunnahabhain	56 Lagavulin	60 Tobermory

The Islands

Inspiring bold John Barleycorn!
What dangers thou canst make us scorn!
Wi' tipenny, we fear nae evil;
Wi' usquabae, we'll face the devil!

—ROBERT BURNS
TAM O'SHANTER

From the Isle of Islay off the southwest coast of Scotland to the Orkney Islands off the north coast, the Islands of Scotland trace a long and scattered arc. Warmed by the end of the Gulf Stream, the Islands generally enjoy moderate temperatures, which are rarely below freezing in the winter. Summers are usually cool. A day without wind and some rain, though, is unusual. Some of the Islands average more than 35 days per year of gale-force winds or stronger, and many of the Islands are washed by more than 60 inches of rain per year. With large quantities of rock and peat, the percentage of the land which is useful for farming or grazing is small.

Island malts tend to be fuller in body and stronger in peat than the Highland and Lowland malts. Islay malts, in particular, are well known for their heavy, almost oily body, and strong peaty flavor. Some people even claim to taste hints of seaweed or iodine. Whiskies from the other islands, though perhaps somewhat less forceful than the Islay malts, still tend to be more full in body and more peaty in flavor and aroma than typical Highland or Lowland whiskies.

What makes the Island whiskies so special is hard to say. Perhaps it is the island peat. Perhaps it is the moist sea air, perpetually blowing across these islands, which imparts something to the whisky as it ages over the years in its porous oak casks. Perhaps it is the pure island water, filtered through the fibrous peat.

Even if we cannot point with any certainty to the cause, we can still enjoy the delightful effects of the Island whiskies.

The Islands are full of history and the subject of innumerable legends. Life on the sparsely-populated islands is arduous. Consider, for instance, problems of transportation. In order for the Isle of Jura distillery to make whisky, its malted barley must be trucked from the Lowlands of Scotland to the lonely outpost of Kennecraig on the Mull of Kintyre. From there it is transported by ferry for a two-hour trip to the Isle of Islay. Finally, it must be ferried once more, this time across the narrow Sound of Islay to the Isle of Jura. The finished whisky, of course, must follow the same course back to the Lowlands, generally to Glasgow, for bottling.

Such remoteness affects the population of the Islands in many ways. Because of their small numbers, schoolchildren customarily board at secondary schools on the mainland and visit their homes on the islands only every other weekend or so. The lack of jobs has also prompted emigration of the young people from the islands to the mainland.

Scattered among the islands are 13 malt whisky distilleries. Twelve of these produce a single-malt whisky. The Port Ellen distillery, on the Isle of Islay, sends most of its whisky for blended Scotch and only on very rare occasions bottles a single malt.

The Isle of Islay (pronounced *eye-la*) must surely deserve the name the Whisky Isle, for she has no less than eight distilleries: Ardbeg, Bowmore, Bruichladdich, Bunnahabhain, Caol Ila, Lagavulin, Laphroaig, and Port Ellen. This is truly amazing when one considers that Islay's population is only around 3,800. From Islay, one of the most southerly of all the Scottish Islands, one can easily see Northern Ireland to the south on a clear day, from whence the art of distilling came to Scotland many centuries ago.

The Isle of Mull is separated from the mainland by the Sound of Mull and the Firth of Lorn and has only 1,500 inhabitants. It supports one distillery, the Tobermory Distillery. Just off the west coast of Mull are the islands of Iona and Staffa. Iona, the first monastic outpost in Scotland, served for many centuries as the traditional burial place of Scotland's kings. Staffa, famous for Fingal's Cave, was the inspiration for Mendelssohn's 'Hebrides' Overture.

The Isle of Skye, which was wrested from the Norsemen in the thirteenth century, is home to the Talisker distillery. This was the headquarters for Bonnie Prince Charlie's Jacobite uprising, and it was to Skye that he fled in 1745, under cover of mist and darkness, never to return. Skye now has a population of 7,340.

The Orkney Islands are really a collection of 73 separate islands with a combined population of 17,000. The Orkneys were visited by the Romans as early as 85 A.D., later colonized by the Norsemen, and came under Scottish rule in 1172. Both of the Orkney distilleries, Highland Park and Scapa, are on the largest of the Orkney Islands, the Mainland Island.

Ardbeg distillery, Islay

Ardbeg
(ISLE OF ISLAY)

About an hour and a half into the ferry ride from Kennecraig on the mainland to Port Ellen on the Isle of Islay, if the weather is tolerably good, the attentive passenger may catch a glimpse of the Ardbeg distillery on the south-east coast of Islay. Its whitewashed warehouses, proudly emblazoned with the name ARDBEG, stand out from the dark green grassy and bracken land rising behind. Ardbeg's pier, for long the only real access to and from the distillery, lies in a partially protected harbor called *Loch an t-Sailein.*

The water for distilling, pure and soft, comes from two lochs uphill and about three miles to the north, Loch Iarnan and Loch Uigeadail. The local peat, of good quality and abundant, is cut and used for the floor maltings at the distillery.

With such resources at hand, it is no wonder that illicit distilling took place at Ardbeg long before the first licensed operation was begun. In fact, the local smuggling operation was so large that the excise officers, fearing for their personal safety, waited until the smugglers had sailed away to make a delivery before moving in to destroy the stills, supplies, and stored whisky.

The first licensed distillery was built by the MacDougall family in 1815. Small at first, the distillery has gradually expanded. It now has two stills and can produce about 300,000 gallons of spirit per year. After many years of private ownership, Ardbeg is now owned and operated by Hiram Walker and Sons.

Although for many years Ardbeg was rarely bottled as a single malt, the distillery is now marketing more and more of its whisky in that form. Bottled at ten years old, it is pale in color, but has the distinctive, rich peatiness of an Islay malt. Not quite as heavy as Lagavulin or Laphroaig, but smokier than, for example, Bowmore, Ardbeg succeeds in combining a full-bodied character with a certain sharpness in its taste. Ardbeg is very good whisky, and a worthy member of the Islay family.

Bowmore distillery, Islay

Bowmore
(Pronounced *bow* **mor** *ay*)

(ISLE OF ISLAY)

Bowmore distillery is on the eastern shore of Loch Indaal on the Isle of Islay. Once the main anchorage for Bowmore, this sea loch has now been silted is no longer navigable. Bowmore is the oldest of the eight licensed distilleries on Islay. It is reputed to have been established in 1779 by David Simpson. In 1837, ownership passed from the last of the Simpson family to James and William Mutter Stanley P. Morrison Ltd acquired the distillery in 1963.

The town of Bowmore, which wraps around the distillery, is the largest on Islay. It boasts an old and architecturally interesting round church which was recently repaired extensively.

The unusual pagoda-roofs of the malting towers serve as more than distinctive decoration at Bowmore. Using peat cut locally, Bowmore still malts most of its own barley on the premises. It is one of the few distilleries which still uses traditional floor malting. In this process, the moistened barley is spread out on the floor. Then, to prevent it from over-heating and to ensure even development during germination, workmen periodically turn the barley with large, flat, malting shovels. Four stills now operate at Bowmore, providing a capacity of nearly one million gallons of spirit a year.

Bowmore is available as a single malt at twelve years old. It is not as full of peat as some of the Islay malts, nor is it as full in body as most other Islay malts. It is medium-bodied, and some people describe it as "gentle and fruity" but it also has elements of the salt-sea air of Islay. It fills the whole mouth; and there is a long, pleasant finish. Its subtle complexity can be quite pleasant; but there can be no mistaking that its origin is the Isle of Islay.

Bowmore is also now available in older forms. We sampled the 1969 vintage, bottled at around 22 years, aged in sherry casks. The peatiness is still delightfully strong. In the mouth, it is a bit meatier than the 12-year-old, with more malt and oak tones. There is a slightly odd accent in the middle of the flavor that we found unattractive. But on the whole, it is a well-composed malt.

Bruichladdich distillery, Islay

Bruichladdich
(Pronounced *brook* **ladd** *e*)

(ISLE OF ISLAY)

On the west coast of Loch Indaal, just across from Bowmore and north of Port Charlotte, is Bruichladdich. Founded in 1881 by the Harveys, Bruichladdich is the most westerly of all the Scottish distilleries. It takes its name from the Gaelic for 'the little hill by the shoals'. The site provided access to the protected waters of Loch Indaal for receiving supplies and shipping out the finished whisky. It was also near a source of good water for distilling. The building was made of concrete, a new technique at the time.

The Harvey family continued to run the distillery until after the First World War. Following a short silent period, Bruichladdich was bought in 1938 by National Distillers of America, who, in turn, sold the distillery to Associated Scottish Distillers. Ross and Coulter acquired it in 1952 and sold it to A.B. Grant. Invergordon acquired Bruichladdich in 1969. To celebrate its centenary in 1981, Bruichladdich commissioned a book called *The Making of Scotch Whisky*, by Michael Moss and John Hume. They also made a special bottling that year of Bruichladdich single malt.

The distillery was extensively modernized in 1960 and again in 1975. It now has four stills, and a capacity of 800,000 gallons per year. The distillery no longer does its own malting on the premises, preferring instead to have the malting done to its specifications on the mainland and then transported to Islay by ferry.

In addition to modernizing the physical plant, some old traditions have been modified at Bruichladdich. At one time the employees were allowed a certain number of drams of the product a day during their work-shift. This old tradition, which was not confined to Bruichladdich, has been replaced with the practice of giving each employee a bottle of whisky each month, an additional bottle at vacation time, and another bottle at Christmas.

Bruichladdich is available as a ten-year-old single malt. It has a rich, peaty aroma and a forceful, full-bodied flavor with an almost nut-like taste, though it is a bit lighter than some of the other Islay malts. Bruichladdich won two gold medals in 1979 and is representative of the better Islay malts.

Bunnahabhain distillery, Islay

Bunnahabhain

(Pronounced *boon a ha ven*)

(ISLE OF ISLAY)

About two miles north of Port Askaig, on the northeast coast of Islay, lies Bunnahabhain. This distillery, which opens into the Bay of Bunnahabhain, looks across the waters of the Sound of Jura to the three high hills on the Isle of Jura known as the 'Paps of Jura'. Built in 1883, Bunnahabhain has been owned by the Highland Distilleries Company since 1887.

The distillery was refurbished in 1963 and enlarged from two to four stills. It no longer does its own maltings on the premises. The water for distilling comes from Loch Staoisha, high above the distillery, by way of the stream 'Abhainn Araig'.

For long an essential part of one of the most popular blends of whisky in Scotland, The Famous Grouse, Bunnahabhain is also available as a bottled single malt. At twelve years old, its fairly pale color is deceptive. It is a decent Islay malt, well-peated, with a substantial, slightly oily body. It has a light touch of the 'iodine' taste which can be found in many of the Island malts.

Bunnanabhain can also be found in vintage form—a 26-year-old distilled in 1964 and a 21-year-old distilled in 1969.

Caol Ila distillery, Islay

Caol Ila

(Pronounced *kull eel a*)

(ISLE OF ISLAY)

Caol Ila distillery lies on the northeast coast of Islay. Its name is Gaelic for 'the Sound of Islay', the narrow body of water that separates Islay from Jura. Just south of Caol Ila is Port Askaig, where the Caledonian and MacBraynes ferry calls once a day from the mainland, and a smaller ferry shuttles the sparse traffic to and from Jura several times a day.

The distillery was built in 1846 by Hector Henderson, who also owned the Calmachie distillery in Glasgow. It stands at the bottom of a small niche carved out of the high promontories of rocky land which rise around the distillery on all sides except the waterside. The Distillers Company Ltd gained control in 1927, and its subsidiary, Scottish Malt Distillers, took complete ownership in 1930. Thus, Caol Ila is now under United Distillers. With the exception of its warehouses, Caol Ila was completely rebuilt in 1972–74, and the number of stills was increased from two to six.

The water for Caol Ila comes from a small but reliable loch on the high ground behind the distillery, Loch nam Ban. The barley is not malted on the premises, but is done on Islay by Scottish Malt Distillers in the Port Ellen maltings.

Caol Ila is seldom available as a single malt, but the distillery has made available a 15-year-old that is still difficult to find. It is a delightful whisky, with the characteristically strong peatiness of an Islay malt, but in a light, almost flinty way. It is somewhat similar to Lagavulin or Laphroaig, but it is not as heavy or oily in body as these other whiskies. It has a clean, fresh taste which is reminiscent of the salty-sea breezes which blow across Islay. It is a shame that Caol Ila is not more readily available.

Highland Park distillery, Orkney

Highland Park

(ORKNEY ISLANDS)

To the north of the mainland, a ferry ride across part of the North Sea, are the Orkney Islands. While Orkney culture may share more similarities with the Norsemen than the Celtic Scots, they have maintained a long and enduring tradition of Scotch whisky distilling. Kirkwall, where Highland Park is located, was the site of illicit distilling before the end of the eighteenth century. One of the early smugglers in the area was Magnus Eunson, who was not only the proprietor of the illicit local still, but was also a preacher. Tradition has it that more than once, Magnus managed to hide the whisky from the ever-inquisitive Excisemen by stashing it under the pulpit of the local church.

Highland Park maintains its traditional floor maltings. The peat is cut locally and comes from the hillsides rather than the more usual low-lying boglands. Another distinctive feature of Highland Park's maltings is that they add a small quantity of heather into the peat fires while drying the malted barley, imparting the aroma and flavor of heather as well as peat to the finished whisky.

The distillery, which has four stills, stands on a hill, with the peculiar result that it must pump its water uphill to the works, rather than relying on the more usual gravity feed.

Acquired by James Grant in 1888, the present owners, the High land Distilleries, took ownership in 1937.

Highland Park is widely available as a twelve-year-old single malt. Not as full-bodied as most other Island malts, it resembles a Highland malt much more closely than most Island malts. Highland Park has a soft aroma which is not overly peaty. The taste is well-balanced, filling both the mouth and the back of the throat with a smooth, lightly peated warmth. This is followed by a pleasant, lingering aftertaste. Highland Park is a very nice malt whisky.

Isle of Jura distillery, Jura

Isle of Jura

(ISLE OF JURA)

It takes a determined traveller to reach the Isle of Jura. The trip begins with a two-hour ferry ride from Kennecraig on the mainland to Islay—a voyage that is markedly longer in bad weather. Then there is another ferry ride to cross the Sound of Islay before finally arriving at Jura. The less patient person can take a small-plane flight on Loganair from Glasgow to Islay, and catch the ferry from there to Jura.

Jura is perhaps best known for its extensive herds of red deer and its three rocky peaks, the Paps of Jura, which entice naturalists and outdoorsmen to the island for the summer season. Though not much smaller than Islay, Jura has fewer than two hundred permanent residents.

The distillery is in the town of Craighouse, and since there is only one paved road on the island, it is hard to miss. A license for distilling was taken out in 1810 by the Campbell family. Production, though, ceased in 1901 as a result of the whisky glut at that time. In 1958 plans were made to revive the distillery, and an entirely new facility was opened in 1963.

Most of Isle of Jura whisky is used in the blends sold by the Mackinlay company, such as Mackinlay's Finest Old Scotch Whisky and Mackinlay's Legacy. Some, however, is bottled as an eight-year-old single malt. Though Jura is but a short ten-minute ferry ride from Islay across the Sound of Islay, Isle of Jura malt whisky is quite different from that of its neighbors. It is intriguingly somewhere in between a Highland and an Island whisky. Its aroma is medium-bodied, without the iodine or seaweed characteristics which many find in the Islay malts. Its taste, likewise, is fresher and cleaner than most Islay malts. But Jura does have stronger peat tones than most Highland malts, resulting in a body which is substantial without being heavy. All in all, Isle of Jura is a very pleasing whisky.

Lagavulin distillery, Islay

Lagavulin

(Pronounced *la ga voo lin*)

(ISLE OF ISLAY)

Lagavulin distillery is on the south-east coast of Islay, midway between Ardbeg and Laphroaig. Its whitewashed warehouse is visible from the ferry just before arriving at Port Ellen. Lagavulin Bay, which provided sheltered access to the distillery, is formed by a rocky peninsula, near the end of which stand the ruins of Dunnaomhaig Castle, where Robert the Bruce, the great fourteenth-century King of Scotland, who ultimately defeated the English, sought safety after being defeated by the Earl of Pembroke.

Illicit distilling in the area dates back to the 1740s. In the years of legal operation, Lagavulin was actually two different distilleries. One was founded in 1816 by John Johnston. The second was established shortly after in 1817 by Archibald Campbell. The two facilities were joined in 1837. After many changes of ownership, Lagavulin was bought by White Horse Distillers in 1924. Acquired by the Distillers Company in 1927, control of the distillery was given to Scottish Malt Distillers in 1930. Thus, it is now a member of the United Distillers family.

Lagavulin was extensively rebuilt in 1962 and now has four stills. Though it has kept its pagoda-style malting chimneys, its malt is now provided by the nearby maltings at Port Ellen.

Lagavulin rates very highly among the Islay malts. Some even consider it the paradigm of an Islay whisky, if such a thing could exist. Lagavulin is available as a twelve-year-old, though this is becoming increasingly rare. The distinctive peaty aroma is delightfully rich and smooth. The flavor is strong, dry, and less sweet than most Islay malts. It is very full in body with a rich, complex texture of peat and salt sea air which tantalizes the senses. This is a classic among malt whiskies. It is worth spending some effort to find it.

Replacing the twelve-year-old is a 16-year-old version, chosen and aggressively marketed by United Distillers as one of their four 'classic malts'. The 16-year-old has lost some of the freshness of the twelve-year-old; but this is more than made up for by the increased malt and sherry tones that balance the sharp smokiness nicely. This is a wonderfully complex whisky with an extraordinary, lingering finish. One of the best.

Laphroaig distillery, Islay

Laphroaig
(Pronounced *la froig*)

(ISLE OF ISLAY)

Laphroaig is perhaps the most well-known of the Islay whiskies. The distillery lies on Loch Laphroaig on the south-east coast of Islay, about a mile east of Port Ellen and very close to Lagavulin. Looking east, one can see the Kintyre peninsula of the mainland, and if the weather is exceptionally clear, an edge of Northern Ireland, not many miles to the south.

The first clear record of the Laphroaig distillery is in 1826, when it was under the direction of Donald Johnston, who had the unusual fate of dying in 1847 by falling into one of the vats in his own distillery. The business stayed in the same family until it was acquired by Long John International in 1962. It is now owned by Allied Distillers.

The distillery has been enlarged several times with the total number of stills now standing at seven.

Laphroaig, like Bowmore, still malts a large portion of its own barley. The peat is cut locally, helping to add that special Islay touch to the whisky. (Some say it is the mosses in the peat which make it so special on Islay.) The water for distilling, over which Laphroaig has had several disputes with Lagavulin, comes by way of the Kilbride River.

Laphroaig is widely available as a ten-year-old single malt. The aroma is peaty, though not as much so as, for example, Lagavulin. It has a well-rounded, mellow taste which is even a bit sweet when compared to the sharpness of Caol Ila, Bruichladdich, or Lagavulin. Laphroaig still retains that heavy Islay richness in both aroma and taste. It is our impression that Laphroaig is more mellow than it used to be a decade or so ago. This is particularly evident in the 15-year-old version that is now available, a dram that is considerably less sharp than its ten-year-old sibling. All in all, this is a very nice whisky. In our opinion, the ten-year-old offers a bit more distinctiveness than the more mature bottling.

Scapa distillery, Orkney

Scapa

(ORKNEY ISLANDS)

Scapa shares the Orkney Islands with the Highland Park distillery and lies about two miles from Kirkwall, on the north shore of Scapa Bay (also known as Scapa Flow). Quite near the distillery are the ruins of an old Pictish outpost, dating back several centuries. The remains of a water wheel, which once powered the distillery, still stand in Lingro Burn.

The distillery was built in 1885. It was acquired by Hiram Walker in 1954 and licensed to Taylor and Ferguson Ltd, and is now owned by Allied Distillers.

The water for distilling comes from Lingro Burn. The maltings, however, are not done on Orkney, but instead, the malted barley is shipped from the large Group Maltings in Kirkcaldy which serves a number of distilleries.

Though not easily found, Scapa is available as a single malt at eight years old. Like Highland Park, it resembles a good Highland malt. It has a medium-bodied aroma and a well-balanced taste. It is light- to medium-bodied, with a deep, rich color. A pleasant, though not special, malt. A few additional years in the wood would improve this whisky.

Talisker distillery, Skye

Talisker

(ISLE OF SKYE)

The Talisker distillery, the only distillery on the 'Misty Isle' is not in the town of Talisker, but is in the small town of Carbost, about three miles east of Talisker. Sitting at the edge of Loch Harport, which offers protected access to the sea, Talisker offers a spectacular view of the Cuillin Hills, rising to the southeast. These mountains, famous among Scottish mountain climbers, rise dramatically to peaks as high as 3,257 feet barely two miles from the sea coast.

The Distillers Company first took an interest in Talisker in 1916 and consolidated their acquisition in 1925. John Walker and Sons now market Talisker under the direction of United Distillers.

Talisker has been available at several different ages. The eight-year-old sells well, but is still quite fiery. The twelve-year-old, on the other hand, is smoother and more mellow, allowing the complexity of the whisky to be appreciated. Curiously, the twelve-year-old used to be more easily available in the United States than in Scotland and England, where the eight-year-old is standard. Since 1989, ten-year-old Talisker seems to have become the norm, as United Distillers now markets it aggressively as one of its "Classic Malts".

Talisker is fairly heavily peated and has the special seaweed tone of many of the Island malts. This is an intense whisky that fairly explodes in the mouth. It is clean, dry, and very well-balanced with an intense, lingering finish. Scottish poets have written favorably of Talisker, and a taste will explain why.

Tobermory distillery, Mull

Tobermory

(ISLE OF MULL)

Tobermory, on the northern edge of the Isle of Mull, is one of the most picturesque of Scottish island villages. Sheltered by forested hills rising behind it, the town curves around the northern portion of Tobermory Bay.

Since it was originally built towards the end of the eighteenth century, the Tobermory distillery has suffered a long series of ups and downs. John Hopkins and Company acquired it in 1890. Tobermory was then taken over by the Distillers Company in 1916 and was closed in 1928. It did not re-open until 1972, when it was re-established as the Ledaig Distillery; but that venture folded in 1975. In 1979, the distillery re-opened as the Tobermory Distillery once again, but it was soon closed again and remained closed until 1990. In May 1990 production began again, and in not too many years we should see a single malt directly from the distillery.

In the meantime, a single malt, under the designation 'Ledaig', is available through the Gordon and MacPhail Connoisseur's Choice series. Our sample had no age identified, but was distilled in 1972. This is a full-bodied whisky, with a strong, robust nose. The flavor is dry, with a distinct taste of peat and a hint of the wooden cask. It goes down with a bit of an edge to it.

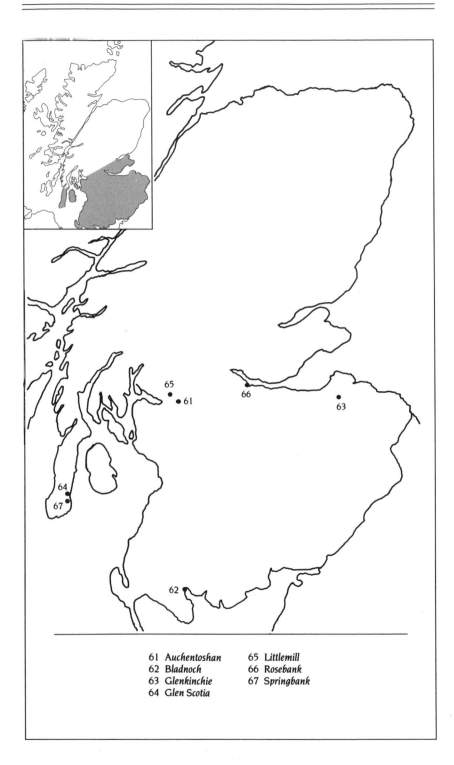

61 Auchentoshan   65 Littlemill
62 Bladnoch   66 Rosebank
63 Glenkinchie   67 Springbank
64 Glen Scotia

The Lowlands
and Campbeltown

Then let us toast John Barleycorn,
Each man a glass in hand;
And may his great posterity
Ne'er fail in old Scotland!

—ROBERT BURNS
JOHN BARLEYCORN

The Lowlands, with their relative openness offering the opportunity for conquest, have served as the battleground for much of Scotland's history. In the first century A.D. the Romans pushed the Celts as far north as the Grampian Mountains. The Romans were soon pushed back to the Tyne and Solway firths, where the Emperor Hadrian built his famous wall, 70 miles from coast to coast. At the beginning of the fifth century, the Romans departed, leaving the North Britons in the Lowlands and the Picts in the north. In the next few centuries, there was a continuing struggle between the Picts, the North Britons, the invading Scots (bringing the art of distilling from Ireland) and the Angles from the south. The ninth century brought occasional forays from the Norseman (though they kept mostly to the Islands). After the Norman invasion of 1066, Norman influence soon extended throughout the Lowlands.

The Lowlands contain the bulk of the population of Scotland. The region also contains the bulk of the economic and political life of the country. Glasgow is its largest population center and the focus of heavy industry. Edinburgh is the paper city, both literally—as a manufacturer of quality paper—and figuratively—as the seat of governmental administration and money and banking. Intellectually, the Lowlands have provided such towering figures as John Knox, David Hume, Adam Smith, and Robert Burns.

Several factors have led to the development of the Lowlands. The presence of coal and iron ore fed the industrialization of the Clyde Valley, providing the foundation for urbanization on a large scale. This urbanization has been fueled by the immigration of unemployed people from the Highlands as well as more recently from Ireland. Navigable waterways, most notably the Firth of Forth and the Firth of Clyde, provided transport routes. In addition, the relative gentleness of the geography made overland roadways a possibility. Finally, the very soil itself is more conducive to rich and productive agriculture than the Highlands.

The Lowlands are most involved in the whisky industry by way of blending. Most of the large blending concerns do their business out of the Lowlands with Glasgow, Edinburgh, Perth, and Dundee serving as important blending and exporting centers. A large part of the grain whisky that goes into commercial blends is also produced in grain distilleries in the Lowlands. Nevertheless, there are several malt distilleries in the Lowlands that do bottle a portion of their whisky for sale as a single malt.

The single-malt whiskies of the Lowlands seem to reflect the gentleness of the terrain and the refinement of the Lowland society and culture. They tend to be lighter in body and aroma than their Northern and Island counterparts. In some cases, that difference is attributed to a triple distillation process used instead of the Highland and Island practice of only double distillation. Because of this quiet gentleness, Lowland malts have rarely been regarded with the same respect as the Highland and Island malts; yet a light, soft, Lowland single malt might be just the right thing for a cool, misty April evening when the grass is damp and the smell of spring foliage is in the air.

Quite different from the industrialized urban belt of the Clyde and Forth valleys is the Campbeltown region. The Mull of Kintyre is a long peninsula on the very southwest coast of Scotland, reaching southward toward the north coast of Ireland. While driving to a Lowland distillery, one is likely to see numerous industrial centers along the way; but when driving down the coast of Kintyre to Campbeltown at its southernmost end, one is more likely to find seals sunning themselves on the rocky shoreline.

Warmed by the Gulf Stream, Campbeltown's weather is quite different from the eastern parts of Scotland. With care, some subtropical flora, such as palm trees, can be maintained, for while the summers are not very warm, neither are the winters very cold.

Campbeltown was originally a town of two industries—fishing and distilling. Both industries have declined in recent decades. From a record high of 32 distilleries, Campbeltown now operates only two, Glen Scotia and Springbank.

The Campbeltown malt whiskies are of a kind all their own. They reflect in their character the sea water that virtually encircles the area. They tend to be full-bodied, somewhat oily whiskies, not at all like true Lowland malts. They bear some resemblance to some of the Island malts, particularly those of the Isle of Islay which is not very far from Campbeltown; but they also reflect a good bit of the soft, rounded lightness of a good Irish single-malt whisky, for Ireland is only about 30 miles distant.

Auchentoshan distillery, Strathclyde

Auchentoshan

(Pronounced *awk en tow shun*)

(OLD KILPATRICK, STRATHCLYDE)

Auchentoshan, which lies about ten miles north and west of Glasgow, was originally built in 1825. After numerous changes of ownership, it has finally come to rest in the hands of Eadie Cairns and Company. Its close proximity to Glasgow meant that during the Second World War, Auchentoshan was badly damaged by German bombing. After extensive repairs and rebuilding, its capacity was increased in the late 1960s from under 200,000 gallons to over a million. Auchentoshan is now owned by Stanley P. Morrison and Co., owners of the Bowmore distillery on Islay.

Auchentoshan is unusual in several respects. For example, though it is technically a Lowland whisky, since the distillery lies just south of the Highland line, its brewing waters are actually drawn from Highland territory. Another distinctive feature of Auchentoshan is its very uncommon triple distilling practice. Instead of relying upon the usual double distillation (the wash still and the spirits still), Auchentoshan whisky goes through *three* separate distillations. It is to this process that its notable smoothness is attributed. The resultant whisky is highly valued by blenders.

The distillery operates a well-organized visitor hospitality program, which includes an educational tour of the distilling works and a visit to the company-operated gift shop as well as a 'hospitality' stop to sample Auchentoshan's single malt.

The single malt is bottled in a variety of forms—ten, twelve, 18, and 20-some years of age. The triple distillation produces a twelve-year-old that is light, clean and soft, without any harshness. The lightness of its body should not be misconstrued as absence of body. Indeed, Auchentoshan has a *good* body. The 20-odd year-old (exact age unspecified) that we sampled is a 1966 vintage. This has a fuller, more complex aroma than the twelve-year-old, with more of a hint of sweetness. The body is a bit more substantial, though still relatively light. There is a touch of woodiness, but we did not find it offensive as it seemed a little more oaky than musty, just a bit intriguing. Personal preferences, though, might differ here. Auchentoshan favorably stands out among Lowland whiskies.

Bladnoch distillery, Wigtownshire

Bladnoch

(BLADNOCH, WIGTOWNSHIRE)

Bladnoch Distillery, is located just outside of Wigtown, on the river Bladnoch, from which it gets its water. Bladnoch is one of Scotland's older distilleries, established in 1818 by Thomas and Andrew McClelland. It is also the most southerly of all the distilleries—making it the lowest of the Lowland single malts. The Martyrs' Monument which commemorates the Covenanters is also located on a hill just outside Wigtown.

Although the distillery was closed from 1938 to 1956, it has been owned and operated by Arthur Bell and Sons since 1983 and thus is now part of United Distillers. The distillery underwent an expansion and modernization in 1957 after its re-opening and again in 1965. Most of the whisky produced by Bladnoch goes into blending; however, it is available as an eight-year-old single malt which is mainly available only regionally in the Galloway region of Scotland but which can occasionally be found now in the United States. Quite recently, we have also spied a 25-year-old version. Eight-year-old Bladnoch has a rich, full bouquet. The flavor has a distinct taste of peat although the body is a bit thin. This whisky does not go down as smoothly as the better Highland malts, but it is certainly one of the better Lowland malts and should be tried by any connoisseur of single malts.

Glenkinchie distillery, East Lothian

Glenkinchie

(Pronounced *glen kin chee*)

(PENCAITLAND, EAST LOTHIAN)

Founded in 1837 by a farmer named Rate in one of the most productive farming districts of Scotland, Glenkinchie lies not very far east of Edinburgh, near the coast of the North Sea. It takes its name from the valley where it is located—the glen of Kinchie. Later in the 1800s, the distillery was closed and served instead as a sawmill. But with the phylloxera blight in France, increasing demand for whisky led to the re-opening of production. The distillery was substantially rebuilt and expanded when it joined Scottish Malt Distillers in 1914. In the late 1960s, Glenkinchie took the lead in establishing a museum devoted to malt whisky, which with the help of many other distilleries has evolved into a most enjoyable and educational aspect of a visit to Glenkinchie.

For most of its productive history, Glenkinchie has been used almost exclusively for blending. However, a marketing move of United Distillers in 1989 introduced ten-year-old Glenkinchie as a single malt to the retail market. It is a typically clean and light Lowland malt. A slightly flowery aroma, with but a touch of peat, is matched with a light body. It fills the mouth nicely, with a light, fragrant finish.

Glen Scotia distillery, Argyll

Glen Scotia

(Pronounced *glen sko shya*)

(CAMPBELTOWN, ARGYLL)

Glen Scotia was established by the Galbraith family in 1832. It is the only distillery which we know of that is reputed to be haunted. It is said that one of its previous owners, a Mr. McCullum, when he had been swindled of a substantial sum, drowned himself—and his ghost still occasionally walks the distillery. It is now owned by Gibson International.

After a long period of silence, Gibson plans to bring Glen Scotia back into production. To economize, however, much of the whisky will be aged at Glen Scotia's sister distillery held by Gibson, Littlemill. What sort of whisky is produced by aging a Campbeltown in a traditional Lowland district remains to be seen.

Though quite difficult to find, Glen Scotia is available as a single malt, bottled at five and eight years. Like its neighbor, Springbank, Glen Scotia's malt is somewhere between an Islay and an Irish malt, though Glen Scotia is noticeably lighter than Springbank. It is fairly peaty and full-bodied in aroma. Its body is soft, malty and substantial, with just a touch of that peculiar Campbeltown oiliness.

Littlemill distillery, Dunbartonshire

Littlemill

(BOWLING, DUNBARTONSHIRE)

Littlemill distillery is generally recognized as one of Scotland's oldest distilleries, though it is difficult to tell exactly how old it really is. Originally, Littlemill was a brewery, and there is some record that Littlemill provided accommodations for some of the earliest excise officers in 1772; however, exactly when the switch from brewing to distilling took place is unknown. Ownership of the distillery went through a variety of different people until Duncan G. Thomas, an American, acquired it in 1931. Barton Brands, Inc., of Chicago, later took over and ran the distillery until 1982 when Amalgamated Distilled Products took over Barton Brands and all of its subsidiaries. Now, like Glen Scotia, it is held by Gibson International.

Most of the whisky produced at Littlemill goes into blending. Both House of Stuart and Highland Mist use Littlemill malt whisky in their blends. Littlemill also produces a five-year-old and an eight-year-old single malt. Although classified as a Lowland malt because of the location of the distillery on the Firth of Clyde not far from Auchentoshan, Littlemill uses Highland peat and water from the Kilpatrick Hills nearby. Also, earlier in this century, Littlemill converted from triple-distillation to the more common double-distillation process, and in that regard resembles Highland distilleries more than the Lowland ones.

The eight-year-old Littlemill is a smooth whisky with a rich bouquet and a definite taste of peat. The taste is pleasant enough, though one tends to taste it towards the front of one's mouth and in the nose. The taste has a certain sweetness to it. The body is a bit thin leading to a very light finish that leaves one a bit disappointed in having been less than fully satisfied.

Rosebank distillery, Stirlingshire

Rosebank

(FALKIRK, STIRLINGSHIRE)

Situated near Falkirk on the banks of the canal that connects the Firth of Clyde and the Firth of Forth, the Rosebank site is reputed to have been used for distilling as early as 1798. The distillery was officially established in 1842 by James Rankine. It stayed in family hands until 1894 when it became a publicly held corporation. After the crash of the whisky market at the turn of the century, Rosebank merged with five other companies to form the Scottish Malt Distillers Ltd. It is now operated by United Distillers. Using triple distillation rather than double contributes to Rosebank's light, Lowland character.

Bottled as an eight-year-old single malt, Rosebank is a fairly good whisky. It has a good body in both its aroma and its taste and compares well to other Lowland malts.

Springbank distillery, Argyll

Springbank

(CAMPBELTOWN, ARGYLL)

Springbank Distillery can justifiably lay claim to several marks of distinction. At one time there were as many as 32 different distilleries in Campbeltown, but following the closures in the 1920s Springbank was one of only two Campbeltown distilleries to survive. When Glen Scotia was closed, Springbank was for a while the only Campbeltown distillery that remained in operation. Springbank is also one of the very few distilleries which is still owned by descendants of the founders, J. and A. Mitchell, who first founded the distillery in 1828. It is also one of very few distilleries which still does its own floor maltings, and it is one of only two distilleries which does its own bottling on the premises (the other is Glenfiddich).

Perhaps the most distinctive feature of Springbank's process which contributes significantly to the quality of its product is that the whisky, as at Auchentoshan and Rosebank, is put through three instead of the usual two distillations. The beginning and end of each distillation—the foreshots and feints—are routed to a separate pot still where they are distilled again. Usually, the foreshots and feints are collected and saved to be added to the low wines in the next distillation.

As a single malt Springbank is bottled as a twelve-, 15-, 21-, 24-, and occasionally 50-year-old. Twelve-year-old Springbank is an unusually smooth and mellow whisky. It is pale in color since no coloring is added in the process. The nose is well-balanced, delicate, and very fragrant. The flavor is full and round, with a touch of peat and a medium body. There are tones of salt and a Campbeltown oiliness. The 21-year-old has a rich, gold color. The aroma is full, smooth, and complex, with peat alongside a slight woodiness. The flavor is rich and fills the mouth with peat, malt, wood, and a touch of heather. This is an excellent whisky.

Also available is a 24-year-old at cask strength of 58 percent. With the exception of the sherry casks in which it was aged, this whisky was produced by materials all taken from within eight miles of Campbeltown. The barley, peat, and coal were all local, as of course was the water. This whisky is quite a treat. A superb, rich, complex aroma captures one's attention. The body is big, firm, full, and well-rounded. There is a beautiful balancing of malt, peat, wood, and salt-sea. After an initial sip, try splashing just a touch a water, and note the differences in aroma and taste. Then decide how you most enjoy it.

Springbank has also begun to market 16-year-old Longrow, an old-fashioned Campbeltown single malt, distilled, aged, and bottled by Springbank. This is unusually good. Longrow is intensely, though not excessively, smoky. The smokiness fills the nose and mouth, yet without cancelling out other tones that nicely balance off the peatiness. The result is an extraordinarily rich and distinctive whisky; one that bears some resemblance to Lagavulin. If you like smoke in your single malt, then Longrow is one that really deserves your attention.

How to Organize a Whisky Tasting

And they hae taen his very heart's blood,
And drank it round and round;
And still the more and more they drank,
Their joy did more abound.

—ROBERT BURNS
JOHN BARLEYCORN

Anyone who has participated in a wine-tasting will understand that tastings serve several purposes. Such gatherings, when well planned, provide an opportunity to experience and learn more about wine; they can also be the occasion for good food, conviviality, and engaging discussion. In this regard, what is true of wine is no less true of single-malt Scotch. Learning to discriminate among the various different single malts and becoming familiar with the regional differences (and even the differences within regions) requires a fair amount of experience of tasting and comparing the different brands, and doing this with friends and colleagues adds greatly to the process by providing an opportunity for comparing the different reactions and opinions of different people. And, it is more fun!

A Scotch tasting will not only broaden your knowledge and experience with single-malt Scotch whiskies, it will also make you much more aware of your senses of smell and taste as you concentrate intensely on the 'nose' and taste of the whiskies. You will learn that it is actually possible to discriminate among different aspects of taste, and you will stretch your vocabulary (as we have done in writing this book) to try and find the words or expressions to capture the sometimes marked and sometimes subtle differences amongst the different single malts. Consider a Scotch tasting as an exploration—an opportunity to discover and enjoy new experiences.

It is certainly possible to have single-malt Scotch tastings at any time of the year; however, we feel that the cooler months are best

suited to really enjoy the full range of malt whiskies in a tasting. Since the colonial period, the English have joked about using gin to ward off malaria in the tropics, but using Scotch whisky to break the chill of a cold, nasty winter evening is no joke. A single-malt Scotch tasting party is about the only kind of party we know of where the host or hostess might really appreciate having bad weather.

There are two ways to approach an evening of tasting. One is to have the tasting before dinner; the other is to save the tasting as a form of after dinner entertainment. To enhance the national origins of single-malt Scotch, the food for the evening can be chosen to highlight some of the delightful food products for which Scotland is famous. Salmon, smoked or fresh, is an obvious choice. Also appropriate would be lamb (an animal almost ubiquitous in Scotland!), beef (an excellent product of the Highlands), and game, especially venison and pheasant. Encourage your guests not to smoke. Some crackers, and cheese if you wish, will help guests to clean the palate between whiskies. If your plan is to conduct the tasting after dinner, make sure that your guests understand the special treat which is in store for them so that they may wisely limit their alcohol consumption during the early evening. (Making sure that guests understand the evening's plan can also help avoid unfortunate misunderstandings. At one Christmas party, a very helpful guest used eighteen-year-old Macallan which had been decanted for tasting to mix eggnog. Everyone was very complimentary about the 'fantastic' eggnog, but there was no Macallan left for tasting! It's a good thing that this guest is such a good friend, and he is still sheepishly apologetic.)

Planning the Tasting

There are several things to consider when planning a single-malt Scotch tasting—some are very practical matters while others are more matters of personal preference and style. Later, we will offer some suggestions about particular single malts to use.

Size

First, keep it simple and small. Our experience is that using four (or no more than five) single malts allows people to focus on the different whiskies (and to remember their experience better after the party). Also, keep the number of people small—usually no more than ten, and certainly no more than a dozen. The focus of everyone's attention and conversation during the time of the tasting should be on the whisky, and having more people just means that it is that much more difficult to keep the occasion focussed. You don't want people standing in a corner talking about business or world politics during the tasting. Invite your friends and acquaintances who are adventuresome and who enjoy new experiences. Finally, written invitations with some very brief explanation of what you intend to do will allow people to come in the proper frame of mind (just a sentence or two will do).

Whisky Selection

Next, you must decide how to select the different single malts to taste. (Here there may be some constraints imposed upon you by the availability and cost of different single malts where you live.) There are different ways to organize your selection of the whiskies. As a good general introduction to single-malt Scotch, you can choose one from each of the different regions which we have discussed in this book—the Highlands, Islands, and Lowlands, and you can also separate Campbeltown from the Lowlands. It is also possible to focus on a single region. For example, there is great variety to be found in the single malts from the Islands. Most of the whiskies from Islay differ significantly from Jura (from the Isle of Jura) or Talisker (from the Isle of Skye) or either Highland Park or Scapa (from the Orkney Islands). There are other possibilities as well. One might choose to sample whiskies of different ages from the same distillery, or focus only upon specially aged whiskies, such as 21- and 25-year-old single malts.

Educating Your Guests

We suggest that a tasting be an opportunity for people to learn something about whisky, Scotland, and themselves. Begin the tasting by telling people something about single-malt Scotch and how it differs from blended Scotch. You don't need to give a long-winded lecture; just a few words of explanation will help people appreciate the differences. Stress that single-malt Scotch is made from no grains other than malted barley and comes from a single distillation by a single distillery. Blends, on the other hand, even premium blends, are only 10–40 percent malt whisky; and most people are surprised to learn that the malt portion of blends can be a combination of up to 30 or 40 different single malts. Having a map of Scotland to point out the different regions (and to locate the particular distilleries and their locations later in the tasting) is also a good idea.

Next, explain to your guests something about the whiskies they will be tasting. You need not, and indeed should not, tell them the specific names of the whiskies yet; but it is helpful for your guests to know that they will be sampling from the different regions (and the general characteristics of the regions included), or if you have chosen to focus on a specific region, what that region is and its general characteristics.

Materials

A traditional Scottish whisky glass is a short glass with straight or slightly flared sides. Some tasters prefer brandy snifters, since they serve well to concentrate the aromas. Do not use tall, 'highball' glasses. Since bottles are different colors, sometimes the first good look you get at the color of the whisky is when you pour it. Using fine cut crystal glasses means that the crystal picks up the light through the whisky and rolling the whisky in the glass and holding it up to a light allows the color of the whisky to dance off facets of the crystal.

We have a preference for blind tastings. That way, people are less likely to frame their reactions by prejudging the different whiskies. One way of arranging this is to cover the labels on the chosen bottles, but since there may be distinctive bottles involved, a safer route is to decant some of the whisky into a pitcher or decanter. Finally, pencil and paper are useful to guests who wish to record their impressions of the tastings. We encourage our guests not to be secretive and not to consider this as a contest among whiskies. Open discussion can help bring to everyone's attention aspects of the tasting that otherwise might be overlooked; such discussion can also help everyone find adjectives to describe their experiences.

Guiding the Tasting

Especially if your guests are new to whisky tasting, it will help to guide them through the appropriate steps. All tasting should be done with 'neat' whisky, or perhaps, in some cases, by adding just a touch of bottled spring water. Try not to use ordinary tap water since the chemicals in the water will mask the subtle variations in the flavors of the different single malts. Also, for tasting, just a wee dram will do nicely—half an ounce is all you need for a proper tasting.

There is no reason for anyone to overindulge, and remember that your guests will have to get home safely. The tasting of a whisky can be broken down into three parts.

Pre-Tasting

Color is the first thing to note. There is no 'standard' color of Scotch whisky. Some are as pale as ripe wheat while others are as dark as the burnished copper pot stills that produced them. The differences are determined by the kind of cask in which the whiskies are aged, how long they are aged, and whether caramel has been added.

The aroma, or 'nose' as it is called by professionals, should be the next aspect to garner your attention. Cup the bottom of the glass in your hand as you hold it to warm the whisky slightly. This helps the evaporation so that the full bouquet of the spirit is released. The aromas of the different single malts will vary considerably—from light to rich, sweet to dry, 'clean' and simple to 'heavy' and complex. The most important thing to look for in the 'nose' of a quality single malt is a smooth, mellow aroma. The aroma can still be strong or even potent—after all, you're sniffing a distilled spirit—but it should never be harsh or pungent.

Tasting

As you taste the whisky, take a sip, hold it briefly in the mouth. Don't slosh it around. Doing so is melodramatic and unnecessary. Concentrate as the flavor fills your mouth and nostrils. Swallow the whisky slowly but completely to receive the full effect, and notice, as the taste in the mouth disappears, how the warming continues down the throat. Does the taste fill your mouth? Or does it touch upon only certain areas, such as the tip of the tongue or only in the back of the mouth? We prefer a whisky that awakens most of the mouth rather than only a small part. Is the flavor thin, or full in body? Is it sweet or dry? Or perhaps nutty? Is the taste smooth and mellow, or harsh and sharp? Can you taste the peat used in malting the barley? Can you taste the differences in the peat from Islay—with heavy mineral deposits from the sea—from the peat from the Highlands with just a touch of heather? Is the flavor complex, having many different enjoyable aspects? Are the different sensations nicely bound together, or are they disparate in the mouth?

Finish

The final part of the taste is the 'aftertaste' or the 'finish' which lingers—sometimes for quite a few seconds—and can differ noticeably from the initial taste. Some single malts finish quickly with little or no aftertaste while others linger nicely and finish very slowly with a pleasant aftertaste which adds considerably to their enjoyment.

Remember that there is a wide range of responses—even from the so-called experts—and each person will have his or her own way of evaluating and describing a single malt, and each person will have his or her favorites. We have certainly disagreed between ourselves on more than one occasion and found this to be part of what makes the enjoyment of single-malt Scotch such a rich, rewarding experience to share with friends.

Some Recommended Tastings

Here are some suggestions of specific single malts to use for a tasting.

An Introductory Tour

Springbank (Campbeltown)

Auchentoshan (Lowland)

Macallan (Highland)

Laphroaig (Island)

First, let us assume that availability and price are major considerations. In some areas of the country, it may not be possible to get the selection and variety which are now available in most major metropolitan areas (which certainly opens up new opportunities for souvenirs when you or relatives or friends travel); so, let us concentrate on the more readily available and less expensive single malts. There are still wonderful, different possibilities and difficult choices to be made. Let us confine ourselves to four single malts. One way of doing this is to choose a single malt from each of four regions (separating the Campbeltown single malts from those of the Lowlands). You could start with a Campbeltown single malt—Springbank is probably the most widely available (and, in this case, very representative as well). The Lowland single malts are not so widely distributed in the United States as those of the Highlands, but we have seen Auchentoshan and Bladnoch in different parts of the country, and either of these would be a good choice for a Lowland spirit. If a single malt from either the Lowlands or Campbeltown cannot be found in your area, Glenfiddich, which is a widely available Highland malt that has a lightness resembling the Lowland malts, may be substituted. Choosing just one single malt from the Highlands may be very difficult—there are so many excellent choices to be made. However, considering both availability and price, the Macallan twelve-year-old would be an excellent selection, as would Glenfarclas. The Island single malt which would give perhaps the greatest contrast to the Highland malt whiskies and which is also widely available is Laphroaig. Its heavily peated flavor contrasts sharply with the mellow, clean taste of Macallan or Glenfarclas. But Laphroaig is heavier and a bit sweeter than other Islay malts. Lagavulin and Caol Ila are our favorites and would make excellent selections if you can find them.

There are, of course, many possible variations on this theme. Another way to combine the tasting of four single malts is to have just one representative of the Lowlands and Campbeltown— Springbank will do nicely—and then separate the Islay single malts from the other Island malts. So, you could have Springbank, Macallan or Glenfarclas, Laphroaig or Lagavulin or Caol Ila from Islay, and either Talisker from Skye or Highland Park from the Orkneys. Both Talisker and Highland Park are more similar to a typical Highland single malt than they are to the Islay whiskies.

The Highlands

Glenmorangie or Clynelish

The Glenlivet

Glenfarclas or Knockando

Royal Lochnagar or Glengoyne

This gives an opportunity for real connoisseurs to have a tasting with single malts from only one region. With the Highlands, it is easy to separate the Speyside or Glenlivet distilleries from the Northern and Eastern ones. So for a good variety of contrasting single malts— all from the Highlands—you could include Glenmorangie or Clynelish (both Northern) along with The Glenlivet, and either Glenfarclas or Knockando (both Speyside) and Royal Lochnagar (Eastern) or Glengoyne (Perthshire).

The Islands

Bowmore or Bunnahabhain

Laphroaig or Lagavulin

Talisker

Highland Park

Island malts offer more possibilities than a newcomer to single malts might imagine. The Islay malts are perhaps most distinctive, but there are quite noticeable differences even amongst them. Laphroaig and Lagavulin are most heavily peated, while Bowmore, Bruich-laddich and Bunnahabhain are relatively lighter. Caol Ila is one of our favorites, but it can be quite difficult to find. Then Jura, Talisker, and the Orkney malts (Highland Park and Scapa) are quite different from the Islay malts.

Various Ages

Glenfarclas Twelve-Year-Old

Glenfarclas Twelve-Year 104 Proof

Glenfarclas 15-Year-Old

Glenfarclas 21- or 25-Year-Old

One is often able to find single malts of different ages, even from the same distillery. To explore the effects of aging on whisky, one could devote an evening to different offerings of different ages. Glenfarclas, for example, offers two different twelve-year-olds, a 15-year-old, a 21- and a 25-year-old. Glenturret may be harder to find, but it offers not only different ages, but also single malts that have been aged in different kinds of barrels, new oak versus bourbon oak versus sherry oak.

The Premium Tasting

Springbank 21-Year-Old

The Glenlivet 21-Year-Old

Glenfarclas 21-Year-Old

Macallan 25-Year-Old

If you are prepared to spend more money, and to hunt down some harder-to-find bottles, you could have a tasting of the 'premium' single malts—those aged 15 years and beyond. These can be excellent and most interesting whiskies, often capable of upstaging the finest of brandies and cognacs. We have done this with the 21-year-old Springbank, 25-year-old Knockando Extra Old Reserve, the 21- and 25-year-old Glenfarclas, the 21-year-old The Glenlivet, the 18- and 25-year-old Macallan, and the 25-year-old Aberlour-Glenlivet.

This blind tasting can convert many a fan of cognac! Be forewarned, however, that though it may be a connoisseur's delight, this tasting slate could prove to be an expensive form of entertainment.

Two Evenings of Malt Whisky

To help you on your way toward your first single-malt Scotch tastings, we shall conclude with suggestions for how to organize two different evenings. (Don't overlook the opportunity to celebrate such holidays as St. Andrews Day, commemorating the patron saint of Scotland, November 30th, and the famous Robbie Burns Day, January 25th, celebrating the birthday of Scotland's most illustrious poet!)

It would be hard to think of a Scottish-inspired evening without including smoked salmon. Traditionally, and quite easily, it is served on toasted points of brown bread with lemon and a pepper mill at hand. Cock-a-Leekie soup is a well-known traditional dish for which recipes are widely available.

Venison is an admired meat in Scotland. It is increasingly available in the U.S., especially by mail order, shipped frozen. A beef tenderloin could readily be substituted.

Venison with Green Peppercorn-Whisky Sauce

(SERVES 8)

Marinade:

2 garlic cloves, finely minced

2 large onions, minced

2 cups dry white wine

$^2/_3$ cup whisky

4 T. vegetable oil

2 t. salt

1 t. coarsely ground pepper

2 boneless loins of venison of
    around 3-4 lbs. total

Sauce:

$^1/_4$ cup whisky

3 T. crushed green
    peppercorns

1 pint whipping cream

$^1/_2$ cup chicken stock

$^1/_2$ cup undiluted
    condensed beef broth

EVENING ONE
An Introduction to Malt Whisky

Appetizer

Smoked Salmon on Toast Points

Tastings

Auchentoshan (Lowland)
Springbank (Campbeltown)
Macallan (Highland)
Laphroaig (Island)

Soup

Cock-a-Leekie Soup

Entrée

Venison with
Green Peppercorn-Whisky Sauce
with
new potatoes and green beans

Dessert

Cranachan
and
Scottish Shortbread

Have the loins sliced into 8 slices each. Combine all the marinade ingredients and marinade in the refrigerator overnight. (It is easiest to do this in a large, plastic resealable bag.)

Combine the whisky, green peppercorns, cream and stocks and simmer, reducing the volume by about a third. Cover and keep warm.

Remove the venison from the marinade and grill over a hot fire until rare or medium-rare. (If grilling is impracticable, sauté in an oil and clarified butter mixture.)

For each serving, use two slices glazed with the sauce. Offer the remaining sauce at the table.

Cranachan in a traditional dessert, also known as cream crowdie. Our recipe comes from Scottish friends of ours, the Watson family.

Cranachan

(SERVES 8)

Ingredients:

---

1 pint whipping cream

^{1}/2 cup oatmeal (Scottish fine cut pinhead oats are most preferable)

4 T. confectioners' sugar (more or less to taste)

2 cups fresh raspberries or blackberries, otherwise 1 t. of vanilla extract

---

Toast the oatmeal in a heavy frying pan until it is slightly browned. Whip the cream until stiff, adding the sugar while whipping. Fold in the oatmeal and berries or vanilla. Allow to set, refrigerated, for several hours.

EVENING TWO
A Highlands Tasting

Pasta

Scotch Pasta

Entrée

*Trout with
Wild Mushroom Sauce
with
snow peas and julienned carrots*

Dessert

*Poached Pears
with orange zest and Drambuie
followed by
Assorted cheeses and crackers*

Tastings

*Glenmorangie or Clynelish
The Glenlivet
Glenfarclas or Knockando
Royal Lochnagar or Glengoyne*

The first course of pasta is a slightly enlarged version of a recipe offered by the Scotch Whisky Information Center. It is a delightful tribute to both smoked salmon and Scotch whisky.

Scotch Pasta

(SERVES 8 AS AN APPETIZER)

Ingredients:

11–12 oz. pasta (rigatoni or shells)
3 shallots, finely chopped
2 T. butter
6 oz. smoked salmon, chopped
11–12 oz. heavy cream
¹/₂ cup Scotch whisky
3 T. lemon juice
Chopped parsley, preferably the flat leaf Italian parsley

Cook pasta according to the directions of the package until al dente. Drain well. Meanwhile, sauté shallots in butter in a large skillet until tender but not browned. Add salmon; sauté 2 minutes, stirring constantly. Add cream; stir in the whisky and lemon juice. Cook gently for about 2 minutes to thicken slightly, stirring often. Pour over pasta. Transfer to warm serving plates. Garnish with lemon wedges and sprinkle with parsley.

While the quality of Scottish salmon is legendary, one should not forget that Scottish streams are also full of trout. For this dinner, we use one trout per person, filleted and skinned. The fillets are then baked in a broth of fish stock, a bit of dry white wine, and wild mushrooms. Other possibilities might be a nice lamb dish, or pheasant (if it can be found).

For the cheese board, we make an effort to reflect the finer cheeses of Britain, Scottish cheeses, like the Orkney (smoked or unsmoked) are still difficult to find in the U.S.; but English cheeses can easily be had. In addition to a cracker assortment, one might also include some Scottish oatcakes, which are an excellent accompaniment to both cheese and whisky.

Whenever we taste single-malt Scotch, our thoughts are inevitably drawn to the Scotland that we have visited so often—the windswept Islands, the damp moors, and rugged hills of the Highlands, and the verdant rolling terrain of the Lowlands. We fondly recall the many distilleries we have visited and the friendly Scots who helped us along our way. We hope that you find your exploration of single malt Scotch as enjoyable as we have found our research.

Further Reading

There are a few other books on single-malt Scotch whisky. These include:

Brander, M. *The Essential Guide to Scotch Whisky*. Edinburgh: Canongate, 1990.

Jackson, M. *Michael Jackson's Complete Guide to Single-Malt Scotch*. Philadelphia: Running Press, 1990.

Milroy, W. *Wallace Milroy's Malt Whisky Almanac*. New York: St. Martin's Press, 1991.

Wilson, J. *Scotland's Malt Whiskies*. Gartocharn: Famedram, 1975

There are several very fine books about Scotch whisky in more historical and general terms. These include:

Barnard, A. *The Whisky Distilleries of the United Kingdom*. Harper, 1887.

Cooper, D. *A Taste of Scotch*. New York: Deutsch, 1989.

Cooper, D. *The Century Companion to Whiskies*. London: Century, 1983.

Daiches, D. *Scotch Whisky: Its Past and Present*. New York: Deutsch, 1969.

Gunn, N. *Whisky and Scotland*. London: Routledge, 1935.

Lockhart, R.B. *Scotch*. London: Putnam, 1959.

McDowall, R.J.S. *The Whiskies of Scotland*. John Murray, 1967.

Morrice, P. *The Schweppes Guide to Scotch*. Dorchester: Alphabooks, 1983.

Saintsbury, G. *Notes on a Cellar Book*. London: Macmillan, 1920.

Moss, M. and J.R. Hume, *The Making of Scotch Whisky*. James and James, 1981.

Seton, M. *The Whisky Distilleries of Moray*. Moray District Libraries, 1980.

Simpson, B., A. Troon, S.R. Grant, H. MacDiarmid, D. Mackinlay, J. House, and T. Fitzgibbon. *Scotch Whisky*. London: Macmillan, 1974.

Wilson, J. *Scotland's Distilleries*. Gartocharn: Famedram, 1975.

Index

Page numbers of the main entry for each distillery are noted in **heavy type.**